LANGUAGE AND LITE[RACY SERIES]

Dorothy S. Strickland, F[...]
Celia Genishi and Donna E. Alve[...]

M000017695

ADVISORY BOARD: *Richard Allington, Kathryn Au, Bernice Cullinan, Colette Daiute, Anne Haas Dyson, Carole Edelsky, Mary Juzwik, Susan Lytle, Django Paris, Timothy Shanahan*

continued

For volumes in the NCRLL Collection (edited by JoBeth Allen and Donna E. Alvermann) and the Practitioners Bookshelf Series (edited by Celia Genishi and Donna E. Alvermann), as well as other titles in this series, please visit www.tcpress.com.

Language and Literacy Series, *continued*

Newsworthy

—

Cultivating Critical Thinkers, Readers, and Writers in Language Arts Classrooms

Ed Madison

Foreword by Renee Hobbs

TEACHERS COLLEGE PRESS

TEACHERS COLLEGE | COLUMBIA UNIVERSITY

NEW YORK AND LONDON

Published by Teachers College Press, 1234 Amsterdam Avenue, New York, NY 10027

Grant funding for Digital Skills Workshop received from the Morse Center for Law and Politics and University of Oregon School of Journalism and Communication.

Library of Congress Cataloging-in-Publication Data

Madison, Ed (Journalism teacher)
  Newsworthy : cultivating critical thinkers, readers, and writers in language arts
    classrooms / Ed Madison.
    pages cm. — (Language and literacy series)
  ISBN 978-0-8077-5687-4 (pbk. : alk. paper)
  ISBN 978-0-8077-5688-1 (hardcover : alk. paper)
  ISBN 978-0-8077-7405-2 (ebook)
  1. Language arts (Secondary) 2. Journalism--Study and teaching (Secondary) 3.
  Critical thinking--Study and teaching (Secondary) I. Title.
  LB1631.M353 2015
  428.0071'2—dc23   2015021471

ISBN 978-0-8077-5687-4 (paper)
ISBN 978-0-8077-5688-1 (hardcover)
ISBN 978-0-8077-7405-2 (ebook)

Printed on acid-free paper
Manufactured in the United States of America

22 21 20 19 18 17 16 15   8 7 6 5 4 3 2 1

For my parents and family. My dad remains my number one role model, and memories of my mom continue to guide me.

Contents

Foreword

When I was in high school, I took a journalism class that changed my life. It wasn't much of a school newspaper, to tell you the truth, but it was still an amazing learning experience. It was just after the resignation of Richard Nixon and there was a great spirit of optimism about the role of journalism in advancing the ideals of American government as we approached the 200th anniversary of our nation. Participating as a student reporter, I felt like I was truly part of the democratic process.

Working on the student newspaper, it was a real treat to explore my world through interviewing and observing. I got to collaborate with a team of people who cared about me: they actually valued my writing and proofreading skills. Plus, it was a thrill to see my name in print and learn new professional vocabulary words like *byline, pull quote,* and *subhead.* Most importantly, as a teenage student reporter, I acquired a form of social power by talking with teachers, school leaders, and staff about timely issues facing our school and community. I deepened my level of concern about the need to find solutions to social, political, and economic problems.

During my college years at the University of Michigan, working at the *Michigan Daily,* I really learned how journalism could make a difference in the world. It was there that I saw firsthand the power of the news media to reflect and shape social reality—and where I first fell in love with the big ideas embedded in communication, media studies, and education, igniting a lifelong passion that stands at the intersection of these fields.

Journalism education is the original form of inquiry learning. Student journalism programs offer tremendous opportunities to learners to advance communication, critical thinking, and collaboration skills. It first began in the 1920s as progressive educators aimed to make learning more relevant to the new immigrants entering public high schools. Students must tackle issues of ethics in striving for fairness, accuracy, and balance— and issues of representation, deciding how to depict the people in their communities. By practicing the responsible use of literacy as a form of social power, they develop leadership competencies and gain confidence in self-expression.

Of course, English language arts educators have long been teaching with and about radio, film, magazines, news media and advertising. By the 1960s, Marshall McLuhan led a generation of educators to appreciate that print and visual media wasn't just a delivery system for educational content: They were reshaping communication, expression, and learning. It was then that the term *media literacy* was dedicated to the proposition that all people need the opportunity to both critically analyze and create media. By the 1980s, with the explosion of the 500-channel cable television universe in our living rooms, a group of educators came together as a learning community through a shared belief in expanding the concept of literacy. We wanted to connect new forms of "writing" via creative student media production to new forms of "reading" through a critical examination of the forms of media that most required sustained and in-depth analysis: news, advertising, and entertainment. This book you are reading documents one branch of the vast and complex ecosystem of contemporary media education: Ed Madison calls it *journalistic learning.*

Journalistic learning naturally connects home, school, and community in a way that is authentic and meaningful. Today, expensive technology tools are not required to create and share print, visual, sound, and digital media messages. Free blogging software, smartphones, and YouTube provide easy access to the technical resources to create many forms of media. Thanks to important work in the field by language arts, social studies, school librarians and media & technology educators, students are gaining opportunities to create media as part of their coursework. Undoubtedly, more American middle- and high school students are creating video documentaries in 2015 than at any other time in human history.

That's why it's actually quite ironic that today's students have more First Amendment freedoms outside of school than inside the journalism classroom. The continuing legacy of the Supreme Court's 1988 ruling on *Hazelwood vs. Kuhlmeier* gives school administrators the legal right to censor student journalism. Each year, hundreds of cases of this kind of legal censorship occur. Thankfully, wise educators can help prevent these problems through effective communication with their school leaders; organizations like the Student Press Law Center help students raise public awareness about the importance of enabling students to learn firsthand about the scope and limitations of their rights and responsibilities as U.S. citizens.

When students create media, it can ignite their intellectual curiosity. That is another reason why secondary educators themselves must continue to work to expand the concept of literacy for an information age. This book gives you resources to help you advocate for media education in your school and community. Such advocacy can be surprisingly effective. When the Common Core State Standards (CCSS) were being developed, media literacy educators advocated noisily for its inclusion using classic advocacy approaches. What we learned from the advocacy process is that educational reform is evolutionary, not revolutionary. Our efforts resulted in this one key sentence: "To be ready for college, workforce training, and life in a technological society, students need the ability to gather, comprehend, evaluate, synthesize, and report on information and ideas, to conduct original research in order to answer questions or solve problems, and to analyze and create a high volume and extensive range of print and non-print texts in media forms old and new." As a result of advocacy, the Common Core State Standards now encompass an evolved conceptualization of literacy.

You, dear reader, are part of this evolution. You've chosen to read this book because you are seeking to engage students in relevant learning that connects classroom to culture and community. In *Newsworthy*, Ed Madison offers many vivid and compelling examples of the creative ways that teachers are embedding journalistic learning into the language arts classroom. The remarkable teachers you will meet in the pages of this book are doing their best to advance student journalism in a digital age.

Eric Newton, formerly of the Knight Foundation, once explained that "the digital age has changed almost everything about journalism: *who* a journalist is; *what* a story is; which media provide news *when* and *where* people want it, and *how* we engage with communities. The only thing that hasn't changed is the *why*." Ed Madison is working in this robust tradition. He brings many years of experience as a professional media producer to the practice of teaching and learning; his insights make for compelling reading. For example, you will learn more about the work of Esther Wojcicki, the high school journalism teacher whose boundless energy and dedication has influenced a generation of students at the legendary Palo Alto High School, right in the heart of Silicon Valley. I have always wanted to meet Esther, and despite our many shared interests in journalism, media, technology, copyright, and education, our paths have never crossed. But thanks to this fine book, Esther's imagination and her deep love of teaching and learning leap off the page.

In *Newsworthy*, Ed Madison also captures the perspectives and the instructional practices of a variety of other high school media educators working in urban schools. These teachers have far fewer resources than Esther, but they do their work with just as much effort, compassion, enthusiasm, and talent. What inspiring people they are!

In the pages that follow, you will also learn how college and university faculty and students can collaborate with high schools to develop media education learning communities. Such university–school partnerships represent important approaches to advancing media education through partnerships that support professional development and community service. As you read this book, you will gain practical insight in how to use the power of journalistic learning to engage students to develop vital literacy competencies that support their cognitive, social, and affective needs.

—Renee Hobbs,
Harrington School of Communication and Media,
University of Rhode Island

Preface

It is likely that some part of your morning was spent catching up with the outside world through media. Whether through traditional news sources or social media, most people instinctively want to know what the world was up to while they were asleep. From war zone tragedies to celebrity trivialities, as a culture we value news. Yet the significant role of journalism in our lives can easily escape us—especially as educators. We may simply take it for granted.

While some research suggests that millennials are not as engaged in news and politics as baby boomers (Poindexter, 2012), other findings indicate that young people find news important but prefer nontraditional sources (American Press Institute, 2015). Moreover, older adults sometimes fail to realize that young people have a rich variety of interests that are all their own. This book asserts that adolescent concerns provide teachers with a rich and largely untapped reservoir from which to ignite student engagement. Young people who are encouraged to write about their intrinsic interests are not motivated by grades or a desire to please. They write because they care. By emphasizing deeper exploration of nonfiction genres the Common Core State Standards (CCSS) provide teachers with an opportunity to engage students in ways that speak to their lived experiences. Journalistic reading and writing assignments can open new doors to self-expression, personal reflection, and academic growth.

How do we get more students to care about learning? That is a critical question teachers ask daily as they face increasing demands from parents, administrators, and policymakers who are dissatisfied with the present state of public education. I argue that teaching strategies that attempt to "get" students to do anything are fundamentally flawed. Engaged students naturally embrace the process of learning, whereas some of their peers may appear to resist instruction. A critical question is: What distinguishes the first group of students from the second? We cannot discount the fact that many young people are burdened by socioeconomic setbacks that can impede their progress, yet some students rise above those challenges. Why? These are the fundamental questions that drive the research behind this book—seeking to unlock the keys to student motivation that can transcend personal circumstances and transform lives.

In spring 2010, through the wonders of social media, I was invited to serve as a panelist at a journalism conference at Stanford University. I was a first-year doctoral student in search of a dissertation topic, and the panel's focus on innovation, journalism, and education was aligned with my research interests—making my decision to accept quite easy. Seated next to me on the panel was a language arts teacher and four of her energetic journalism students from Palo Alto High.

Given that the school is situated across the street from Stanford's campus, I expected these students to be impressive. Surrounded by the corporate offices of Facebook and Google, Palo Alto is one of the nation's wealthiest and most intellectually elite communities. However, these students were not just a predictable by-product of privilege. Beyond smart, they were poised, confident, thoughtful, and genuine.

Their teacher was Esther Wojcicki. She told me that Palo Alto High School is credited with having what is likely the largest scholastic journalism program in the country. With more than 500 of their 1,800 member student body participating, they produce eight distinct publications mostly managed by student staffs.

As I explore in Chapter 2, when Wojcicki began teaching English at the school in 1984, the program was floundering, with just 19 students participating. As a former journalist, she believed that many of the profession's practices would provide pedagogical and psychological benefits for her students. Wojcicki noted that adolescents come to school with curiosities and concerns that are not often addressed in their coursework. They are managing parental and peer pressures and are shaping their identities—often without a forum for reflection, discussion, and debate. The results of her efforts validated her beliefs; Wojcicki found that her students were intrinsically motivated to write about their everyday experiences. Also, publishing their work led students to make a stronger commitment to the learning process. They were no longer writing solely to get a good grade or to please their parents. Rather, they were discovering an inner ability to use words to inform and influence their community.

Wojcicki and her colleagues did not invent high school journalism. It has a long history, and as you will discover, numerous schools have developed highly successful programs. However, in many schools journalism exists as the after-school "club down the hall" or as an underfunded elective. The distinction is that Wojcicki and her team placed journalism front and center in their school's curriculum. Many of the journalism teachers also teach general and Advanced Placement English Language Arts (ELA) courses, and journalism strategies inform their pedagogical practices in all of these courses. They have created a culture on the Palo Alto High School campus where the "cool kids" are involved in journalism—and the results are demonstrated by higher levels of participation, productivity, and achievement. The Palo Alto High School program consistently wins top honors in national scholastic press competitions, and their graduates excel in college and in their careers.

As I learned more about Palo Alto High School's program, more questions came to mind. Was it an anomaly? Or was there something worthy of deeper inquiry, something that could inform communities of teachers and students who struggle to meet learning objectives and function outside the insulated boundaries of privilege? This book seeks to answer these questions.

I spent 2.5 years studying the Palo Alto High School program and another 2 years interviewing English language teachers across the United States who are producing similar results with their students through journalism. They offer inspiring teaching strategies that educators without journalism training can employ. I refer to these pedagogical practices as *journalistic learning*.

In spring 2014, some colleagues and I applied many of these principles in a week-long boot camp at Roosevelt High School in Portland, Oregon. The grant-funded project focused on teaching digital storytelling skills to students with limited previous exposure to new technology. We documented an observable transformation in the student participants with video cameras and created online modules and lesson plans to benefit teachers everywhere through a dedicated website, DigitalSkillsWorkshop.com.

The timing of this research significantly coincides with broader acceptance of new, albeit controversial Common Core State Standards. The CCSS were introduced in 2010 and, as of 2015, have been largely adopted by 43 states. As *Newsworthy* will demonstrate, journalistic learning is uniquely aligned with the English Language Arts Standards that call for teachers to place more emphasis on nonfiction texts and digital literacy skills. Within these pages you will find workable and affordable solutions, as well as resources for professional development. You will discover that journalistic learning principles can be easily applied in a range of English and language arts classrooms, even in challenging economic circumstances.

Chapter 1 explores the commonly used terms *student engagement* and *critical thinking* to get beneath the surface of what these terms seek to describe. It also defines *journalistic learning*, looking more closely at the theoretical frameworks and research foundations that inform the book. Chapters 2 and 3 draw from extensive fieldwork and interviews with teachers and students across the United States who are experiencing substantial benefits from journalistic learning strategies. Chapter 4 looks at how this pedagogical approach works across contexts and benefits a broad range of students from diverse backgrounds. Chapter 5 chronicles our research team's effort to apply and expand on our discoveries in a weeklong initiative at Roosevelt High School in Portland, Oregon. It also explores new and affordable approaches to teacher training, as educators seek to integrate more media and technology—as prescribed by the Common Core. The conclusion looks to the future and opportunities for further research and action.

You can find updated resources and videos at NewsworthyBook.com.

Acknowledgments

Special thanks go to my family for their enduring support. I'm grateful to Esther Wojcicki, Paul Kandell, Ellen Austin, and other faculty members at Palo Alto High School and their students, as well as members of the National Council of Teachers of English (NCTE) and the Journalism Education Association (JEA), who allowed me to study their work. Additionally, thanks go to Emily Spangler, my editor at Teachers College Press. Her insights, encouragement, and responsiveness were invaluable throughout this process. Special thanks go to my academic mentors, including Tim Gleason, Julie Newton, Ron Beghetto, Kim Sheehan, Leslie Steeves, Renee Hobbs, Carol Stabile, Jerry Rosiek, Deb Morrison, Pat Curtin, Scott Maier, John Russial, Tom Bivins, Carl Bybee, Bish Sen, and Janet Wasko, as well as to my amazing colleagues Karla Kennedy, Mark Blaine, Lisa Heyamoto, Dan Morrison, Rebecca Force, Alex Tizon, Héctor Tobar, Tom Wheeler, Torsten Kjellstrand, Sung Park, Wes Pope, Peter Laufer, Lauren Kessler, Gabriela Martinez, Tiffany Gallicano, Deb Merskin, Kyu Ho Youm, Chris Chavez, Andrew DeVigal, Mike Fancher, Donna Davis, Kelli Matthews, Jon Palfreman, Dan Miller, Troy Elias, Nicole Dahmen, Laurie Phillips, Lori Shontz, Charlie Butler, Steven Asbury, Shan Anderson, and Gretchen Soderlund. Sources of inspiration and guidance include Michelle Swanson, Matt Coleman, Randy Kamphaus, Art Pearl, Joanna Goode, Ross Anderson, and Terri Ward. The Morse Center for Law and Politics and University of Oregon School of Journalism and Communication (SOJC) funded the Roosevelt High School Digital Skills Workshop initiative. I must also acknowledge Maya Lazaro and our journalism school's support staff. Finally, I thank our amazing students who are shaping the future.

CHAPTER ONE

In Search of Student Engagement and Journalistic Learning

Student engagement is among the most discussed topics in education. But what does it really look like, beyond buzzwords? How can teachers create rich classroom experiences for students that bring conceptual notions to life in more meaningful ways? This, in essence, is the point of this book.

As educators, we want to stimulate deeper levels of learning. It is tremendously satisfying to look out onto a class of students who are attentive and clearly invested in completing assignments or collaborating with peers. Especially rewarding is sensing that we are reaching students who may otherwise be easily distracted, prone to restlessness, or less responsive than their peers.

Fundamentally, in language arts we want students to read and write well. We also want to rouse curiosity, stimulate thinking, and foster understanding. This relates to another common buzzword: *critical thinking*. For many educators, it also remains an elusive concept.

This chapter delves beneath the surface of these buzzwords to offer secondary school educators tangible teaching strategies informed by the practice of journalism. Although journalism is well established within English language arts (ELA), it is often only offered as an elective or extracurricular activity structured as a school newspaper. I argue that journalistic learning offers ELA teachers a broader reservoir of educational resources that are often overlooked. I will define journalistic learning and explore its theoretical and research foundations. I will also specify how journalistic learning supports key objectives stated in the CCSS.

WHY JOURNALISM MATTERS

Journalism informs our understanding of current affairs and popular culture. Yet many teachers consider it a foreign discipline, in some way separate from ELA. In fact, journalism was a launching pad for a number of America's most celebrated authors, including Walt Whitman, Mark Twain, Ernest Hemingway, John Steinbeck, Katherine Anne Porter, Richard Wright, Robert Frost, and James Agee (Fishkin, 1985). Today, journalism can be a significant resource for ELA teachers and learners that develops the skills fundamental to meeting the CCSS. David Coleman, one of the principal architects of the Common Core, says students should "read like a detective, write like an investigative reporter" (Coleman, 2011, p. 4). His inference points to one of the challenges of our times. Teachers are charged with preparing students for a world that is significantly different from the one they experienced during their formative years. In 2010, Google's executive chairman, Eric Schmidt, famously asserted that every 2 days humans create as much information as they had between the dawn of civilization and 2003 (Siegler, 2010). Half a decade later, wearable and sensor-enabled devices are exponentially increasing the amounts of data at our disposal. Detectives and investigative reporters share common traits. Both are trained to ask tough questions, dig beneath the surface, and distinguish between facts and fraud. These are fundamental skills students need to navigate successfully in an increasingly uncertain world.

Sarah Nichols, vice-president of the Journalism Education Association, asserts, "Student media is not only '21st century English' but the very essence of the new Common Core: rigorous and relevant skill-based standards with emphasis on the 4Cs of communication, collaboration, creativity and critical thinking" (Nichols, 2014). The Common Core encourages a broader mix of nonfiction- and fiction-based texts to prepare students for college and career placement. The primary intent of this book is to provide a compass and a road map for reaching that objective through journalism-based methods.

Some may question the usefulness of "journalistic" forms of education, citing closures and cutbacks in traditional publishing as indicators of a profession and practice that are in decline. Undertaking journalistic assignments may inspire some students to pursue the profession; however, that is not the intent of this work. Rather, it is to illustrate journalism's ability to benefit a much broader population of students.

Further, I maintain that concerns about journalism's demise are erroneous. Nicholas Lemann, former dean of the Columbia School of Journalism, notes how the rapid growth of digital media is changing the means of distribution, not the demand for information (Moynahan, 2012). Eric Newton, formerly a senior adviser at the Knight Foundation, best articulates why journalism skills are so essential, stating, "The world can now tweet, blog, take pictures, and more. Every workplace in America needs clear digital communicators. . . . To lead in any field—law, business, non-profits, government—you need to be able to communicate" (Newton, 2013).

Journalistic learning is an approach that resonates and achieves results with 21st-century students. It catalyzes creativity, an essential skill that is enhanced by providing students with opportunities for self-expression, rather than forcing them to memorize facts (Ravitch, 2010; Zhao, 2012). This is a generation that is growing up with pocket devices that can beam images and video around the globe in an instant. It seems commonsensical that media be embraced more rigorously as a tool to improve education. Yet economic challenges and philosophical differences are often roadblocks. Learning how other educators overcome these hurdles helps.

DEFINING JOURNALISTIC LEARNING

First, I want to introduce the term *journalistic learning*. Whereas journalism is a professional practice, journalistic learning is a research-based pedagogical approach that borrows strategies from journalism to better engage students in language arts. So, what is journalistic learning? And how does it differ from other ELA pedagogical strategies? Journalistic learning is a term I began using to describe the peer-to-peer and teaching–student interactions I first observed at Palo Alto High School. Rather than participating passively, students took ownership of their education and leadership roles during the instruction. Levels of engagement were significantly higher than I had witnessed in English classrooms elsewhere.

At its core, journalistic learning looks to current events, community concerns, and personal experiences to engage students at the level of their intrinsic interests. It seeks to "meet students where they are," tapping into their rich reservoir of interests. It hooks them on reading and writing about personal and peer concerns, as a precursor to introducing broader, multifaceted, or fictional themes. Journalistic learning acknowledges that adolescence is a critical phase of development for young people, and that many are without healthy outlets for constructive forms of self-expression (Leary & Tangney, 2003). Journalistic practices, which can include identifying newsworthy topics, conducting interviews, and synthesizing information for audiences, engage students as first-person witnesses to matters that are relevant to their lives.

A distinctive aspect of journalistic learning is its emphasis on the power and pedagogical value of publishing student works. Today this enterprise is virtually cost-free, thanks to digital/online platforms such as WordPress, Tumblr, and others. Yet much of conventional classwork centers on assignments handed in for grading for an audience of one—the teacher. In contrast, the journalistic pedagogical approach acknowledges the benefits of writing for a broader audience. When students realize peers, family, and community members will also read their work, they tend to invest more time and energy (Tate & Taylor, 2014). More important, publishing provides students with an empowering platform. They understand that their voices matter. This sense of empowerment has pedagogical value consistent with critical scholarship (Freire, 1970; McLaren & Leonard, 1993). Additionally, written disclosure has been shown to have a therapeutic effect (Pennebaker, 1989), and it supports self-confidence (Farber, 2003).

At first glance, journalistic learning may seem synonymous with inquiry-based learning, a pedagogical movement first popularized in the 1960s (Bruner, 1961; Schwab, 1960), which has regained currency in recent years. Whereas inquiry-based learning can involve writing assignments drawn from Internet research and field trips, journalistic learning engages students at deeper levels. Journalists do not just inquire; they immerse themselves in events, distinguish facts from fiction, and take ownership of telling accurate stories (Harrower, 2013). Journalism, by definition, is a first-person account of an event or occurrence. It requires more than simply surveying the facts. Immersion involves metaphorically diving into your surroundings and absorbing details and nuances others might miss. You must roll up your sleeves, go out into a community and, like a detective, uncover great stories. The immersion process inspires students, as you will see in the chapters that follow.

Journalistic assignments motivate students for the same reasons many of us follow news and popular culture. We instinctively read about news and trending topics because of their relevance to our authentic concerns and intrinsic interests. This in no way negates the significance and inspirational power of great fiction, nor its place in English language arts. By design, journalistic learning taps into students' self-interests as an initial pathway for further exploration of other complex texts. Students benefit from becoming artful at writing both fact- and fiction-based stories. The best fiction convinces readers that it could possibly be true.

Although journalistic learning is informed by critical scholarship, it is more oriented in American pragmatism. The approach takes theory into applied practice that is intentional and objective based. Journalistic learning, as I define it, has four essential elements that form the core chapters of the book:

- *Relevance: Making Assignments Meaningful*—When teachers tie curricular content to contemporary and personal themes, they are better able to engage students in learning. Schoolwork becomes more meaningful when it ceases to be conceptual and can be applied to everyday life. It answers a fundamental question that many students who have "checked out" are inclined to ask themselves: "Why should I care?" When coursework is relevant, students learn to apply ideas to practices. It contributes to the sense-making process.

- *Discovery: Exploring and Interpreting Information*—Humans are naturally inquisitive. Students who are encouraged to explore tend to thrive. Discovery-oriented learning becomes less about memorizing facts and more about uncovering unknowns. Exploration makes learning fresh and interesting.

- *Sharing: Personal Stories, Diversity, and Empathy*—Vibrant communities honor diversity and embrace cultural differences. Socioeconomic challenges should not impede inclusiveness or a commitment that all community members have an opportunity to be heard. Critical to journalistic learning is the practice of publishing. Students give the gift of their perspective on life to their peers and their communities. A transformation appears to occur when young people realize their opinions matter, and when they have an opportunity to share in a public forum. Certainly, young people are already actively sharing online through various forms of social media, but often without guidance from trained educators.

- *Collaboration: Sharing Curricular Power and Digital Technology*—Journalistic learning occurs when teachers and students share power in the learning experience, and when students are no longer thought of as "empty vessels" to be filled. Rather, it occurs when they are acknowledged as self-determined beings with innate talents that can be nurtured. Meeting students "where they are" academically and creating social-situated learning environments allows peers to support one another through collaborative work. Digital technology enhances the ways in which teachers can instruct and students can work together. Yet teachers need support and sufficient opportunities for professional development, and students need access to and knowledge about new tools.

Journalistic learning also supports students in cultivating leadership skills. It trains adolescents to become self-directed problem solvers. They learn to advocate for their beliefs, mentor their peers, and serve their communities. Student leaders work alongside their teachers to develop curricula and co-facilitate instruction. It gives students "voice," respect, and dignity. Student engagement is achieved and maintained when young people are empowered to take ownership of their education and know their contributions matter.

THEORETICAL BACKGROUND

The journalistic learning approach is grounded in well-accepted theory. Journalistic learning is oriented in the constructivist philosophical traditions of John Dewey and Lev Vygotsky, which focus on experience, and is aligned with the self-reflexive values of Paulo Freire and the discursive insights of Michel Foucault.

Dewey (1938/1997) was an early proponent of experience-based learning. Valuing active participation over rote memorization, he wrote, "there is an intimate and necessary relation between the processes of actual experience and education" (p. 7). Dewey observed that optimal learning occurs when students have hands-on opportunities to engage with real-world experiences that are relevant to their lives. His approach became known as progressive education.

Dewey's work is aligned with Vygotsky (1987), an often-cited Russian psychologist whose social learning theories have left an indelible mark on education practice. Key among them is his concept of the *zone of proximal development*, which Vygotsky defined as the gap between students' current capabilities and their potential development through mentoring by teachers or in calibration with more proficient peers (Vygotsky, 1987; Yamagata-Lynch, 2010). *Scaffolding* is a more contemporary term used to describe the types of supportive interactions that can occur between peers in a social context to facilitate learning. It entails structuring classes to be collaborative spaces where students can explore their strengths and weaknesses for mutual growth (Rodgers, 2004; Wood, Bruner, & Ross, 1976).

Freire (1970) acknowledged the cultural capital that students with diverse backgrounds bring to one another in a learning setting. He demonstrated what's possible when disenfranchised peoples learn to value their own voices. In the early 1960s, Freire taught 300 Brazilian sugarcane workers to read in 45 days by encouraging them to honor their native heritage. Although the experiences of field workers in developing nations are dramatically different from those of most American students, many of their concerns are similar. In all cultures, people have a desire to prosper and provide for the basic needs of their loved ones.

In critiques of social conformity, Foucault (1984) also explored cultural influences by theorizing about relationships of power and the role of discourse. For Foucault, discourse was more than just language, in the traditional sense. He broadened his definition to include ways we engage in social practices. Foucault spoke of "orders of discourse," which acknowledges that certain speech is sanctioned and therefore permissible, whereas other speech is not. Teachers speak one way with their students and another with other teachers. Crossing lines of authority risks retribution.

Foucault distinguished further that a process of *normalization* occurs within society through the discursive practice of categorizing, quantifying, and regulating populations. Psychologists, doctors, and educators emerge as authority figures and are thus empowered to pathologize certain behaviors observed in patients and students as "deviant" or "delinquent." Foucault noted that labeling has carried different connotations at different points in history (Ball, 1990). Normalization within education has left nonconformers to be defined as "others"—and, in many instances, classified as abnormal. These children were often identified as "problems." For example, a child in 1895 with learning disabilities would have been considered "retarded," a term commonly used well into the 1960s. Today, both descriptors are considered pejorative and children with mental disabilities are characterized as having "special needs." Foucault asserted that discursive labeling is more than descriptive; it constitutes subjects. Labeling shapes the way we interpret and therefore view the world.

Journalistic learning is also consistent with the work of contemporary scholars, including Henry Jenkins, who speaks of essential new *digital literacies* students need to thrive, and Ernest Morrell, who challenges educators to acknowledge *cultural literacies* inherent in increasingly diverse student populations. Jenkins (2009) uses the term *participatory culture* to describe this new generation that uses digital technologies to create affiliations, through services such as Facebook and Instagram, and for self-expression through such activities as creating video and writing fan fiction. Morrell (2004) advances the belief that educators now face a *demographic imperative*—meaning they must acknowledge the fact that America's classrooms no longer resemble those of yesteryear.

These scholars informed my development of journalistic learning, an approach to introducing nonfiction texts to ELA students in a manner consistent with an emerging emphasis on collaborative learning, media studies, and educational equity.

In addition to the previously noted philosophical theories, my approach has been primarily informed by research-based theories that center on social learning and student motivation. *Situated learning* (Lave & Wenger, 1991) refers to educational settings where students engage in authentic firsthand experiences. Lave and Wenger's theoretical construct begins with the acknowledgment that we are inherently social beings who learn from our interactions. We come to understand common practices through shared agreements about what they mean. For example, though a book on how to interview can describe the process, its reading is removed from the richer face-to-face experience of exchanging questions and answers. In the moment, the unpredictable can and often does occur. An expected answer can inspire a new line of questions—and the lessons learned can be significant. This is situated learning in action.

Wenger (1998) uses the term *communities of practice* to better describe the social configurations we create and organize around given disciplines. Journalists (much like teaching professionals) ideally operate within a "community of practice"—with a shared identity, knowledge base, and approach to constructing meaning. This is exemplified by journalists' adherence to a common code of ethics, shared jargon, and agreed-upon conventions.

The difference in culture between classroom and newsroom communities is quite distinct. In classrooms, students often seek to please a teacher by giving "correct" answers and fulfilling tasks that meet prescribed standards. Although students may work together in groups, fundamentally their aim is to receive the best individual grade. However, in newsrooms, effective journalists learn to advocate for stories they believe matter on behalf of a greater good. Yes, editors give assignments—but reporters are expected to dig for and generate just as many original story ideas. An overarching shared commitment to public interests fuels the process. Thus, journalists often provide a voice for the voiceless and bring awareness to issues of importance that might otherwise be ignored. These same skills of persuasion are an essential aspect of college and career readiness. Teachers of English language arts and their students can borrow and benefit from these practices and experience the rewards of writing for an audience.

Social learning is not the only factor. Educators also benefit from understanding what motivates students to learn. We want to inspire students to be engaged, as opposed to the consequences that can result when they are not engaged. High truancy rates and mass complaints of boredom by students are indicators of a larger problem teachers face—inspiring students to care. This book's work is also informed by motivation theories that address the underlying attitudes and intentions that precede actions. Specifically, *Self-determination Theory* (SDT) (Deci & Ryan, 1985, 2000, 2002) posits that, much like in biology, humans have basic psychological needs that sustain our ability to lead healthy and productive lives. SDT asserts that motivation exists on a continuum, with intrinsic motivation ranked highest, and followed by lower levels of extrinsic motivations. Fundamentally, we are energized by tasks that align with our existing interests. Likewise, we are less enthused by tasks that are tied to some external reward. Further, self-determined people exercise choice in their actions, feel competent about their abilities, and are empowered by the relationships that arise from shared tasks. The theory is based on a substantially large body of work, conducted over 30 years by numerous researchers (Kiemer, Groschner, Pehmer, & Seidel, 2015; Reeve & Lee, 2014).

RESEARCH BACKGROUND

The principles outlined in this book are drawn from 4 years of study, including extensive qualitative fieldwork at Palo Alto High School in Northern California. There, I studied its award-winning journalism program, in which nearly a third of the school's 1,800 students participate. The program is part of the English department and has a portfolio of eight student-led publications, including a newspaper, a lifestyle magazine, a sports magazine, an online news service, a literary magazine, an art and culture magazine, a yearbook, and a daily three-camera newscast. The publications consistently win top honors from the Columbia Scholastic Press Association (CSPA), and the Obama administration has acknowledged the program and the school for its academic excellence.

The community's affluence and its proximity to Stanford University and the corporate headquarters of Google and Facebook might lead many to assume that the school exists in a utopian bubble bearing little resemblance to the rest of America and is therefore an anomalous choice for study. Yet I argue otherwise; I viewed this site as an opportunity to study and learn from "best practices" that can be applied in a broader context. I offer examples of how journalistic learning strategies practiced there are benefiting students in settings that are very different.

There are other compelling reasons the Palo Alto High School story deserves a closer look. It serves an increasingly diverse student body—a segment of which are bused from the economically and crime-challenged adjacent community of East Palo Alto. In 1992, East Palo Alto was characterized as the "murder capital of the world, with 43 homicides among a population of 24,000 people" (WCBS-TV, 2010).

However, UC Berkeley research indicates a 62% drop in the crime rate since that period (Lawrence & Shapiro, 2010). In recent decades, Palo Alto High School's historically White student population has declined to its present level of 57%. The remaining breakdown of students is 21% Asian, 10% Hispanic/Latino, 4% African American, and 8% other (Palo Alto Unified School District, 2012). East Palo Alto's own high school was closed in 1976, due to low enrollments and poor student academic performance. Upon arrival at Palo Alto High School these students of color generally stay within their existing social circles.

This book's qualitative research focuses on field observations that included videotaped documentation of classroom interactions between teachers and students, recorded over multiple sessions. Between September 2010 and October 2014, I made 10 visits to the school for 3 to 4 consecutive days at a time. This included a 3-day trip in July 2011 to observe students who participated in a grant-funded summer training program for minority youths, which is held in neighboring East Palo Alto.

During visits, I followed students into the field to observe their journalistic assignments and conducted one-on-one on-camera interviews with selected students and teachers. Although my fieldwork at Palo Alto High School provided opportunities for immersive study of journalistic learning in action, I also interviewed other educators across the United States who are effectively using these methods, particularly in less affluent communities. Students' names have been changed to protect their privacy.

I conducted a supplementary survey to cover a range of geographical regions, socioeconomic circumstances, ethnic demographics, and type of English class, including both mandatory classes and self-selected journalism and Advanced Placement or honors classes. Participants included 664 students from 10 high schools across the United States. (See Appendix A for more specifics about participants, methods, and results.)

My findings indicated that much of the success I observed at Palo Alto High is potentially attainable in communities of diverse socioeconomic circumstances with students of diverse ethnicities when controlling for school and student demographics (community type, class standing, or socioeconomic status). Students taught journalistic strategies in less affluent communities reported motivational beliefs and learning strategies that were similar to students in affluent communities, challenging presumptions that Palo Alto High's results are an anomaly. ELA students using journalism strategies also reported significantly higher levels of personal growth and sense of self than ELA students not exposed to journalistic strategies (Madison, 2012).

The objective of further research is to investigate what struggling schools can learn from results achieved at schools with stellar programs like Palo Alto High—schools like Roosevelt High School in Portland, Oregon, where, as the book explores, colleagues and I piloted a program based on these methods.

At Roosevelt 84% of students receive free or reduced lunch. Roosevelt ranks among Oregon's poorest high schools (Parks, 2014). Yet language arts teacher Melody Hughes has witnessed journalism's power to engage her students in new ways. Her Advanced Placement (AP) and traditional track English students excel and are better prepared to graduate and move on to college than their peers. Other educators are producing similar outcomes, and their achievements are chronicled within these pages. Their results are also evidenced by previous studies indicating that when young people have opportunities to craft journalistic stories about their lived and shared experiences, they earn better grades and test scores in high school and college than their peers (Dvorak, 1998; Dvorak & Choi, 2009); outperform their peers in college freshman writing assignments (Dvorak, 1988); and make fewer errors in their writing than AP English and honors students (Blinn, 1982). With regard to the achievement gap, minority students with high school journalism experience are shown to outperform minority students without it in 12 out of 15 areas of high school and college comparisons (Dvorak, Bowen, & Choi, 2009).

CONNECTING JOURNALISTIC LEARNING TO THE COMMON CORE

Candice Perkins Bowen, director of Kent State's Center for Scholastic Journalism, says that when the Common Core was first introduced in 2010 many journalism teachers noted they "sounded a lot like what they were doing already" (Bowen, 2014). Journalistic learning also targets key ELA pedagogical objectives. Specifically, it exposes students to more challenging texts and expands reading comprehension. It emphasizes essential writing skills by teaching students to plan, revise, and edit their work—with an audience in mind. It familiarizes students with a broader range of nonfiction genres, including information-based articles, feature stories, profiles, and commentaries. Students learn to separate facts from opinions and that both have an appropriate place. Journalism focuses on concise writing, and its main objective is to be understood. Further, journalistic learning emphasizes effective speaking and listening.

All of the above-mentioned learning objectives are expressly noted in the Common Core, which calls for substantially more curricular emphasis on nonfictional and informational texts. The Common Core's preamble stresses the importance of media, explicitly stating:

To be ready for college, workforce training, and life in a technological society, students need the ability to gather, comprehend, evaluate, synthesize,
and report on information and ideas, to conduct original research in order to
answer questions or solve problems, and to analyze and create a high volume
and extensive range of print and non-print texts in media forms old and new.
The need to conduct research and to produce and consume media is embedded into every aspect of today's curriculum. In like fashion, research and
media skills and understandings are embedded throughout the Standards
rather than treated in a separate section. (CCSS-ELA, p. 4)

Many educators welcome the Common Core, whereas others are
understandably cautious. Although not every state has signed on to the
Common Core, all states have standards that seek to measure and improve student performance. Students who are engaged and think critically will be better prepared to meet and potentially exceed those measures.

Fundamentally, the intent of the Common Core and all academic
standards is to provide teachers with a framework that supports their
commitment to raising student achievement. As the debate continues to
unfold, there is a present need for tools that are aligned with the Common Core while also acknowledging that the commitment to curricular
excellence lives beyond the policy of the moment. Fundamentally, this
book provides specific strategies for educators seeking real and achievable
outcomes that engage students in new ways.

USING THIS BOOK

This book offers inspiring examples from teachers who are making effective use of journalistic teaching strategies that can be replicated by
readers with ease. It shadows teacher–student interactions, allowing
educators to envision how such strategies might play out in their own
classrooms. In each instance, I connect the strategies to specific guidelines found in the Common Core. Even technology-adverse teachers will
discover nonthreatening ways to add media to their instruction, as well
as low-technology options to enrich their teaching.

Each of the remaining chapters begins with a quote, drawn from my
extensive field research of journalistic learning in action. These "snap-
shots" are later explored in greater detail, along with complementary examples from a variety of educators and classroom settings. The chapters
outline specific ways you can draw from the examples cited and tailor
the strategies for your own use. Shaded boxes within the pages of the

chapters feature the correlating Common Core State Standards. You will find invitations to go online to delve deeper into certain topics. You will be directed to videos, instructional resources, and examples of student works that are provided by educators and organizations that advocate for the strategies outlined in this book. The videos offer firsthand accounts from teachers and the opportunity to witness classroom interactions. Finally, each chapter concludes with summaries, key "takeaways," and additional resources. These sections provide actionable strategies, as well as lists of resources to draw from and put to use.

Embracing the self-reflexive nature of interpretive qualitative work allows me to acknowledge my own motivations and to address "why" these issues matter to me. I am a second-generation media professional, in the sense that my dad (now retired) was a trailblazing journalist during the 1960s and 1970s—a time of domestic social unrest. In 1961, he became the first African American to join the editorial staff of the *Chicago Tribune*. He reported on (and knew) Dr. Martin Luther King, Jr., and he covered the first Kennedy–Nixon debate. My mom was an elementary school teacher—and both parents stressed the importance of academic achievement.

Humbly, I have followed in my father's footsteps. I began my media career at age 16 as a high school intern at the CBS affiliate television station in Washington, DC, during the height of the Watergate scandal. At age 22, after graduating from Emerson College in Boston, I was recruited to join the management team that launched CNN.

I was a professional practitioner of media for nearly 30 years before I ever contemplated the theoretical foundations that inform media scholarship. I am now a journalism professor at the University of Oregon, where I have the privilege of engaging each day with highly talented students who are reshaping the field.

Today, media and education converge in new and exciting ways. Students can create and share their stories with peers a world away. I am interested in how that power can be harnessed to transform education. Where do you begin? In order to better connect with students, coursework must be relevant.

CHAPTER TWO

Relevance

Making Assignments Meaningful

My students were bored, and I was [too]—it was really bad. And, I just made a decision: either I was going to have to quit or throw out the textbook. So I threw out the textbook.

—Esther Wojcicki, ELA teacher, Palo Alto High School

Many educators experience conflicting emotions when asked to teach with materials that hold little interest to either their students or themselves. Some teachers compare it to force-feeding and would prefer to toss away learning aids that may be out of step with the times. Textbook publishers do not set out to burden teachers or bore students. Most classroom texts are the result of rigorous and well-intentioned efforts to synthesize complex information in a digestible format—and many succeed. However, teachers and students frequently complain that they want more.

This chapter provides insights on journalistic learning strategies designed to better engage students by making classwork more relevant to their interests and daily-lived experiences. It introduces observations from my fieldwork at Palo Alto High School in Northern California and offers complementary guidelines from other educators who use similar strategies with a particular focus on reading and writing.

At Palo Alto High School first-year students take a language arts class titled Critical Thinking, and by design it has evolved into a course that draws mostly from news-related texts and contemporary nonfiction. However, that was not always the case.

The school is steeped in tradition and recognized for its academic excellence. Founded in 1898, "Paly," as locals know it, is one of the oldest high schools in the region. The school's exterior façade resembles an old Spanish mission. Although the school is located in one of the nation's most affluent communities, many of its accomplishments should not be viewed unobtainable by schools in more challenging settings. There is much to learn from the philosophical views and pedagogical practices found here.

Portable classrooms are scattered among the historic buildings. (Palo Alto High School inaugurated a new Media Arts Center in October 2014. See the concluding chapter for specific details.) "Paly" sweatshirts, pullovers, and blue jeans are the unofficial dress code for students. Another distinguishing factor is the high degree to which journalism is now integrated into the school's curriculum. Nearly a third of the school's 1,800 pupils participate in some form of journalistic learning.

Yet only 19 students were participating in journalism-related coursework when Esther Wojcicki joined the faculty in 1984 and sensed the need to initiate change. Students began calling her "Woj" (pronounced like lodge) after one decided Wojcicki was too difficult to say—and the nickname stuck. Within months she became disillusioned by textbooks and how quickly the content became dated. Wojcicki decided to bring newspapers in to share with her students, and a school-wide shift in emphasis began.

She realized that a key to making learning relevant is starting students with assignments that speak to their intrinsically motivated interests. Wojcicki also understood the significance of peer relationships among her students. Before the prevalence of online news, she used newspapers to introduce students to reading journalistic profiles and later writing their own personality features about classmates. Prior methods emphasized memorization and multiple-choice quizzes. She recalls:

> At that time, there was something called the *Palo Alto Tribune*, and of course the *San Jose Mercury News*, and the *San Francisco Chronicle*. I said, "We're just going to write in the different writing styles, just like you are writing for the professional press." It's interesting—kids liked it! I'd say, "Okay, we'll be writing features," and everyone would have to find a feature story in the paper. It's hard to believe that people don't know what a feature story is. They could not even pick out a personality feature. So it's kind of interesting, they would pick out obituaries. Nope, if it's a personality feature you have to interview the person. They cannot be dead.

Here, Wojcicki is drawing attention to the fact that students often overlook common distinctions most adults take for granted when reading informational texts. Given the predominant emphasis on fiction in traditional secondary ELA courses, many students simply have not had an opportunity to differentiate between varying nonfiction forms. Yet these genres are very similar to styles of informational texts they will be expected to read, understand, and write about in college and in their careers.

Consider your own experiences. Excluding student assignments you may have graded recently, reflect on the wider range of texts you have read in the past 24 hours. It is likely that most of it was nonfiction, including news, reports, memos, manuals, and emails. Reading and comprehending informational texts prepares young people to effectively write informational texts. Familiarizing students with these genres establishes important skills and proficiencies that will serve them throughout life.

Think about the wide range of documents crafted by people we consider to be effective communicators. Funding and support for new initiatives is almost impossible without a persuasive and well-written proposal that advocates for a position or cause. In similar fashion, industries rely heavily on well-researched and well-written business reports to make informed decisions and take appropriate actions. Much like reporting news, statements made in these types of documents must be backed by credible cited sources.

Whereas fiction explores fantasy, journalism seeks to establish facts. Fiction is associated with "pleasure reading," enjoyed at a leisurely pace. In contrast, journalism is associated with "purposeful reading," and we often consume it when we are crunched for time. We seek information that is relevant to our concerns and interests. Thus, news-related writing seeks to get to the point.

Wojcicki acknowledges that today's students are more likely to engage with online sources of information. However, she believes teachers should not discount the kinesthetic value of the printed page, in terms of its adding another dimension of sensory awareness to the learning process.

There is also a more practical reason she uses newspapers: It ensures that students are actually participating in the exercises, rather than surfing the Internet. Printed periodicals are also readily available in even the most financially challenged communities.

Today, the town of Palo Alto has several weekly newspapers that compete for news stories and readers. Wojcicki finds it valuable for students to take turns reading portions of articles aloud. Hearing the articles adds an auditory sensory function to reading that supports visual perception, thereby enhancing comprehension.

JOURNALISTIC LEARNING IN ACTION: READING

A bell signals the beginning of the next period. Students scurry in and take their seats in armchair desks that form a U-shape around the perimeter of Wojcicki's portable classroom. She stands at the head of the room, holding an open copy of this week's *Palo Alto Daily Post*. She's given each of her 40 students a copy of the same issue. She begins reading headlines: "Okay, here's more news: 'Peninsula to Fight SF Tolls,' 'Palo Alto Flooded with Kindergarteners,' and 'Controversy over Power Use Report.' Everybody read these stories and let's talk about them."

Brian raises his hand, and after being called upon he directs his classmates to a front-page headline above a picture of an abandoned building that simply reads "What's that?" It references a foreclosure. "I think the title falsely represents the story," Brian notes. He observes that the headline and photo are provocative and will likely attract readers. However, he believes such tactics do not engender trust. His classmates and Wojcicki agree. She coaches them to distinguish between news stories and feature stories. She explains that news stories generally make up the front section of the paper and conform to certain writing conventions. News stories typically stick to reporting facts that can be substantiated by eyewitnesses and reliable sources. Feature stories allow writers more creative liberties.

Next Wojcicki introduces her students to the *inverted pyramid*, a writing structure used by journalists to provide readers with the most essential facts of story, followed by details of lesser importance (see Figure 2.1). Readers are free to engage with as much of an article as time and attention span dictate.

She notes that the first sentence in news stories is called the lead (sometimes spelled *lede*). Its objective is to reveal the "Five Ws" of journalism: who, what, when, where, and why. Subsequent sections of an article explore each of these areas in greater detail, often also addressing how an event unfolded.

Wojcicki explains to her students that use of contractions is permissible and even encouraged in journalistic writing, primarily to make stories more conversational. "Starting leads with 'There is' or 'There are' is super-boring, and people are just not going to read any further. You have to make interesting leads." (See resources at the end of this chapter for links to examples of leads.)

Celina, a senior at Palo Alto High, notes the differences:

> For journalism, well, there are rules. . . . Like you have to have a lead, there's the inverted pyramid style. But I think even with those rules it's a lot more flexible than creative writing, because in journalism you can just end a story with a quote. There's not really a conclusion—you don't have to sum everything up. It flows more easily, I think, because you're just sort of giving information.

At the other end of the spectrum, journalistic feature stories allow writers to inject more of a personal "voice." There is a license to

Figure 2.1. Inverted Pyramid

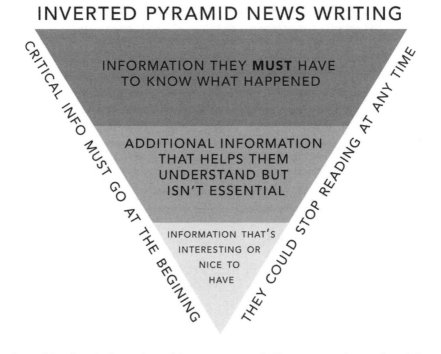

INVERTED PYRAMID NEWS WRITING

INFORMATION THEY **MUST** HAVE TO KNOW WHAT HAPPENED

ADDITIONAL INFORMATION THAT HELPS THEM UNDERSTAND BUT ISN'T ESSENTIAL

INFORMATION THAT'S INTERESTING OR NICE TO HAVE

CRITICAL INFO MUST GO AT THE BEGINNING

THEY COULD STOP READING AT ANY TIME

be subjective, informal, and less structured. Feature stories and opinion pieces incorporate more nuances and challenge students to venture beyond the conventions of the five-paragraph essay.

Several of Wojcicki's students call attention to stories in the news that involve celebrities. "Miley Cyrus was sighted smoking a questionable substance, and a celebrity chef was arrested," Haley states. They note that stories about celebrities are feature oriented but that celebrities can make news when they misbehave. The discussion provides an opportunity to explore what makes stories newsworthy. Celebrities are known to engage in stunts to garner publicity. The class explores whether press coverage of celebrities' misbehaviors may glorify antics that many consider to be socially unacceptable and how such reporting impacts youth.

Discussion moves to a sports story written about the school's football team and its winning streak. Wojcicki observes, "Notice that there is a really good quote from Ryan [one of the players] and it is not quoting facts; it is quoting opinion. They got Ryan to say something interesting. The last thing you want to do is quote a fact."

Students undertake a *close reading* of the text that is purposeful. They learn to hear and later reproduce various writing styles and conventions. At several points in the oral reading exercises, Wojcicki and her students pause to identify and discuss the key ideas expressed by the author and the manner by which they are conveyed.

Wojcicki takes this pedagogical practice a step further to stimulate critical thinking and teach media literacy skills. She asks students to compare how two or more separate news sources may have reported the same story differently. They look for similarities, contradictions, omissions, and above all, accuracy. These exercises teach students to distinguish between factual news stories, feature stories, commentaries, and editorials.

Exercises of this nature teach students not to blindly accept information at face value. They begin to understand that despite best intentions, news reporting is not pure. They also begin to notice which issues draw media attention and which do not. Why do some stories make the front

---

COMMON CORE STRATEGIES

The Common Core asks that high school graduates be able to do the following proficiently:

- Cite strong textual evidence that supports their analysis.
- Identify central ideas and provide objective summaries of texts.
- Analyze how authors unfold ideas, make points, and draw connections.

Bring these guidelines to life by integrating use of newspapers with your students. Although yesterday's newspapers may hold little value for most readers, they can be a great pedagogical resource in the classroom. Arrange for your local newspaper to set aside unsold copies of back issues. Ideally, you'll want all of your students "on the same page," referencing the same issue. Challenge them to make distinctions about how the paper is organized. You can also have students access online sources, including international, national, and regional news websites. Choose an article, and have them take turns reading sections aloud. Pause to take notice of writing style, tone, phrasing, and flow. Have them identify and summarize its central theme. How has the author developed and presented his or her point? Discuss what worked about the article and what may have missed the mark.

Have students note that commentaries, editorials, and other opinion pieces carry a voice of authority. Draw attention to how that authority is effectively and perhaps ineffectively expressed. Ask students how they might take a position and write about an issue of importance in their lives.

page, whereas others are relegated to less prominent positions within a publication? Students begin to assess the accuracy of stories that affect them. To what degree does news media coverage of school budget cuts compare to their lived experience of being students? This is consistent with the Common Core's focus on reading to interpret craft and structure.

Much like Wojcicki, Michelle Balmeo is another secondary-level ELA teacher in the Bay Area who relies on journalistic texts to enrich reading skills. She will have students read passages multiple times to uncover stylistic nuances that may not immediately be obvious. Balmeo refers to these close reading exercises as "X-ray reading," a term she picked up from Roy Peter Clark's *Writing Tools: 50 Essential Strategies for Every Writer*, a book she uses religiously with her English and journalism class students. Much like Superman's special power, X-ray reading involves having students peer through the text. In the book, Clark states, "Beneath the surface grinds the invisible machinery of grammar, language, syntax, and rhetoric, the gears of making meaning, the hardware of the trade" (Clark, 2006, p. 212). Of course another Clark, Superman's alter ego, Clark Kent, is a newspaper reporter, so the reference is appropriate.

Balmeo describes X-ray reading as reading for form rather than reading for content: "Students receive lots of instruction in reading for content. They really struggle, at least at the beginning, with reading for form; like what is this writer doing?" Balmeo said.

Reading well-written works is an essential practice for developing one's own "voice." Artful writers have an ability to captivate readers with words. Good writing has a distinguishable cadence and energy reflected in the words—and is often straightforward in its style and presentation. However, new writers are prone to reach for multisyllabic, complex words with disappointing results. Journalistic writing notably focuses on clarity, and it seeks to be understood.

COMMON CORE STRATEGIES

The Common Core further asks that college- and career-ready students be able to do the following:

- Ascertain the meaning of words and phrases, including figurative, connotative, and technical meanings—and analyze the collective impact of certain word choices.
- Analyze with specificity how an author's ideas or claims are advanced and refined.
- Identify an author's perspective or intent in the text and identify the rhetorical devices used to support his or her perspective or intent.

To build proficiency, select a national or local issue reported on in a newspaper three ways: as a news article, an editorial, and a commentary. Provide all students with the three samples and have them form groups of three. Ask each group member to read all three of the samples quietly to himself or herself. Next, have the members discuss what they gleaned from the reading and compare notes. Did the story stick to reporting the facts? Did the publication's editorial position differ from that of the individual commentator? Which words and phrases stood out? What rhetorical devices were employed to state claims and make arguments, and to what degree were they effective?

JOURNALISTIC LEARNING IN ACTION: WRITING

At Palo Alto High School, Wojcicki guides students to segue from reading to writing news and feature stories. On a different day, she offers students feedback on a writing assignment. They were asked to cover and write a 500-word news story about "Spirit Week," an annual campus-wide competition between class levels that involves costumes and stunts. "Your stories were pretty good—but most were missing good news leads. What is the most important news for Spirit Week? *Who won.* Do you know how many [of you] put that in the lead? Maybe one of you."

"That was me," Brian responds.

"But everyone knows that the seniors won," Ben adds. "They always win."

"You're writing a story for the people who don't know," Wojcicki asserts. She goes to the board and writes in large letters as she states, "Who, what, when, where, why—and, if relevant, how."

A poorly written lead might read, "Spirit Week was a big success again this year, drawing an impressive turnout." It lacks specificity and assumes readers have prior knowledge about the event. A better lead would be "Palo Alto High seniors out-danced and out-dressed fellow students to take first place for the third consecutive year during last week's campus-wide Spirit Week competition." This second example tells us who, what, when, where, and why.

Wojcicki gives her students 10 minutes to revise their leads based on those guidelines before they begin sharing aloud. A well-written lead will capsulize the essence of the story so well that no further reading is required. Collectively, they all note the improvements. Students will have another opportunity to polish the assignment before submitting it for a final grade. This revision process can differ from working with fiction, where embellishments are often added. In contrast, journalistic news writing seeks to strip away excess words in favor of clarity. However, concise sentences do not have to be dry. With practice, students learn to strike an appropriate and effective balance.

More educators are recognizing how broader use of journalistic texts in reading and writing assignments can be beneficial to students. The Journalism Education Association (jea.org) is a national organization committed to supporting educators across disciplines in experiencing the benefits of teaching journalistic genres. Carol Lange is a former ELA teacher who, like Wojcicki, is a longtime member and advocate. She writes monthly "Newspaper in Education" online guides for the *Washington Post* (nie. washingtonpost.com), which are free to the public. Additionally, Lange trains teachers through her Intensive Journalistic Writing Institute (ijwi. net) workshops. Her syllabi have received unanimous approval by the College Board for meeting the stated objectives of the Advanced Placement Language and Composition course requirements. Lange has supported ELA teachers in bridging the knowledge gap since the 1980s. She offers solid resources that demonstrate how journalism and English terms are more aligned than ELA teachers may think. Table 2.1 illustrates how English and journalism terms compare.

Profiles and Autobiography

Lange offers teachers a variety of journalistic writing strategies to engage secondary school learners. One assignment has students write personal profiles about their classmates. To avoid issues of favoritism, students randomly select a peer to profile—further proving that "everyone has a story." Students learn valuable interview skills, including how to build rapport and how to tactfully inquire about sensitive subjects. The assignments often introduce students to cultural traditions that may be unfamiliar—providing opportunities for empathy and mutual understanding. These are tangible skills that build confidence and prepare students for new experiences they will encounter later in life.

Valerie Kibler, one of Lange's protégés, brings 26 years of classroom experience using journalistic strategies to her Advanced Placement Language and Composition students at a high school in Virginia. She underscores the importance of *relevance* in the journalistic approach: "Kids in my AP course find that what they read and what they write is a lot more important to them. Also, what you get as product is so much more interesting to read." In addition to personality profiles about peers, students write autobiographical profiles about their own experiences. With some students, the results can be transformational.

Table 2.1. English and Journalism Terms

English Course Terms	Journalism Terms
Expository Writing	News
Persuasive Writing	Editorial
Narrative Writing	Features
Personal Narrative	Columns

Josh, one of Kibler's 11th-grade students, received a frightening medical diagnosis. Doctors revealed he had testicular cancer, requiring a grueling course of chemotherapy treatments. Rather than keeping his struggle private, Josh chose to write about the experience and to allow it to be published. His touching story inspired classmates to interview his mother and medical experts to better inform readers about the disease. Josh's story moved many of the school's male faculty members to participate in "No Shave November" (no-shavenovember.com), a national cancer awareness campaign where men grow facial hair to acknowledge the hair loss chemotherapy can inflict. Their efforts raised $2,000 toward the cause to find a cure. In this instance, Josh enlightened a community about an issue that is highly relevant—the need to find a cure for cancer.

Josh's story illustrates the value of journalistic teaching methods, and more specifically the potential power of publishing student work. In fact, the importance of publishing is emphasized for every grade level in the Common Core. Submitting work to a teacher for grading seeks to meet his or her assessment standards. Having one's words published requires an additional act of courage and self-disclosure.

The strategies advocated by Wojcicki, Lange, and Kibler correlate with specific guidelines articulated in the Common Core for grades 11 and 12. Specifically, when students research and write about peer or personal challenges, they engage readers by using a reflective process of sharing details, crafted through narrative techniques.

Of course, the choice to publish personal stories must always be left to students. If the subject matter is highly sensitive, students should be advised to consult their parents. However, as demonstrated by Josh's story, a decision to publish can be transformational. Numerous theories explain the dynamics of why.

An aspect of Self-determination Theory (SDT) (Deci & Ryan, 1985, 2000) addresses matters of *emotional regulation* (Gross, 1998), which relates to the processes by which people respond and adapt to emotionally challenging, stressful, or threatening events. Defensive responses involve compartmentalizing, distorting, or making light of matters that are potentially overwhelming (Costa, Zonderman, & McRae, 1985). This is in contrast to nondefensive responses, which involve a willingness to entertain and engage in new coping strategies. Such openness is vital for the successful integration of new perspectives, which can prove more productive (Ryan & Deci, 2000). When integration fails, fearful thoughts may linger, leading to further anxiety and suffering (van der Kolk & van der Hart, 1991).

SDT asserts that effective self-regulation of emotions is tied to one's sense of autonomy, meaning one's sense of choice-fullness about his or her behavior (Ryan & Deci, 2000). Weinstein and Hodgins (2009) note that when troublesome emotions are not processed—meaning they are allowed to stagnate or cycle through the mind—it can adversely affect well-being. Such thoughts may manifest in one's memory as "unfinished business" (p. 351), which can thwart one's energy and sense of vitality.

Pennebaker (1989) asserts that expressive writing about one's challenges frees one from persisting thoughts. Journalistic writing, which can include commentaries and other opinion-oriented articles, requires that the author construct a narrative. This can foster higher levels of understanding and an additional sense of resolution or "closure" (Greenberg, Wortman, & Stone, 1996).

Although some educators might shy away from engaging students in writing about self-reflective or opinion-based subjects, I argue that *relevance* is key to engaging students in substantive learning. Students become and stay attentive when assignments have real meaning in their

---

COMMON CORE STRATEGIES

The Common Core emphasizes that students do the following:

- Write narratives that address real or imagined experiences or events with skill and specificity.
- Engage readers by articulating a problem, scenario, or opinion and its relevance, introducing one or multiple perspectives.
- Employ narrative techniques, such as dialogue, pacing, description, and reflection to develop the plot and/or move the story forward.

Invite students to reflect on an experience or event that holds special meaning in their lives in a 500-word essay written in class. Topics need not be of a sensitive nature but should address a problem or dilemma they may have encountered. Coach them to be mindful of tone, pacing, and perspective. Ask that the essay's final paragraph address how they grew from what transpired. Invite students to read their essays aloud. Encourage feedback. Discuss the narrative techniques employed and whether they were effective. Is it sufficiently descriptive and detailed? Have students listen for cadence. Does the narrative flow?

---

lives. Further, we have an obligation to educate the whole child and to provide transformative learning experiences that offer students opportunities for personal growth.

Reviews

Journalistic writing does not have to always involve highly personal or serious subjects. You may want to start your students with topics less consequential. At Palo Alto High School, Wojcicki also engages students by having them go out into their community to review restaurants and entertainment. Everybody eats and enjoys some form of amusement. This can include fast-food establishments and free cultural events. Calling ahead can gain students complimentary access, especially if the reviews will be published.

The field exercises help students enhance their observation skills and their ability to describe and to form an opinion about their experiences. New students begin working in pairs to best support one another and to ease anxiety. For younger generations of students accustomed to interacting via text messages and social media, field assignments of this nature challenge them to venture outside of comfort zones and to talk with people in person. Wojcicki explains the range of assignment possibilities:

> We also do store reviews and product reviews. If you don't want to take them out of the school you can do website reviews or game reviews. We put kids together and let them write about what they want to write about, and they really want to write. Also, teach them how to tell the truth. So what kind of food is being sold? What's the atmosphere like? What was the service like? No hyperbole—what's really there?

Although it is customary to review restaurants incognito, other assignments require that students place a phone call or pay a visit to schedule a sit-down interview. The process of making these kinds of requests strengthens self-confidence, leadership abilities, and communication skills. The assignments are also relevant because students have a say in selecting the subjects they write about. As the writing exercises progress, secondary-level students develop a deeper sense of the nuances of writing well.

Editorials/Op-Eds

Opinions have their place in journalism. In print or online, there are clearer delineations such as editorials, columns, and op-ed pieces. Editorials generally state the position of a publication's management on any particular issue. Senior staff news analysts generally author columns, and they are at liberty to inject a personal flair. Finally, invited authorities mostly write op-ed pieces on a given topic.

Lange asserts these genres provide invaluable lessons for students:

> An editorial must include a concession to the other side. And you don't give a weak concession. You acknowledge the opposition's strongest argument, followed by your stronger and strongest arguments. In my mind, that's what you have to do in life if you want to be persuasive. It also prepares students for Advanced Placement exam essay questions that ask that they form arguments, having weighed counter perspectives on an issue.

Assigning students to write journalistic reviews, commentaries, and their opinions is aligned with the objectives of the Common Core State Standards for ELA learners.

COMMON CORE STRATEGIES

To be college- and career-ready high school graduates will be proficient at

- Writing evidence-based arguments that support claims and demonstrate valid reasoning
- Developing claims and counterclaims fairly, providing evidence for each while acknowledging the strengths and weaknesses of both perspectives
- Using words, phrases, and clauses to connect, clarifying and providing evidence for claims and counterclaims
- Establishing a formal style, maintaining an objective tone, and following writing conventions, and
- Providing a summation that connects with the argument.

To reach these objectives with students, have class members suggest possible "hot topic" ideas and vote by hand to determine the one they will all write about. The chosen topic needs to resonate with issues they care about. Turn to the headlines to identify possibilities. Examples of issues that work well with secondary students are child labor injustice in developing countries and animal testing by pharmaceutical companies.

Writing effectively about such issues begins with research. Give students an evening or two to investigate the topic, and instruct them to come to the next class prepared for discussion. If Internet access is readily available, coach students to examine a variety of online sources, paying close attention to matters of legitimacy. Is the source journalistic, governmental, or advocacy oriented? Is its ownership transparent? Is it run by a for-profit or nonprofit entity? Does it appear to have an agenda? If so, what is it?

If Internet access is limited, provide students with photocopies of a broad selection of sources on the topics. Post examples on a bulletin board if copying is prohibitive.

Next, have students write a 500–750-word commentary on the issue. Instruct them to address more than one perspective, noting the strengths and weaknesses of each, and acknowledging the evidence. Have them conclude with a summation and closing argument. Consider the best way to have students share their work based on their access to technology.

COMBATING WRITER'S BLOCK

Regardless of the genre, it is not uncommon for students to experience anxieties of starting with a blank page. Language arts scholar Peter Elbow is credited with developing "free writing," a widely adopted technique for helping students unleash their creativity that can be applied to journalistic learning. Students are instructed to begin their writing process with 10 to 15 minutes of nonstop free-form self-expression, with little concern for grammar or spelling. These preliminary exercises are not turned in nor are they graded. Rather, their purpose is to provide students with a "warm-up" period that is free from the pressures associated with more formal writing assignments.

Elbow developed his techniques after reflecting on his own frustrations as a writer and as a writing teacher. At face value, his unorthodox writing instruction methods might seem antithetical to traditional teaching conventions, which are fundamentally linear in their approach. However, his pedagogical philosophy is by no means considered lightweight. Elbow's work is cited more than 1,500 times in the WorldCat library database, and his credentials are formidable. He is an Oxford-trained scholar who pursued graduate studies at Harvard before earning his Ph.D. at Brandeis University. Elbow taught at Massachusetts Institute of Technology and currently is a professor emeritus of English at the University of Massachusetts, Amherst.

Elbow's method emphasizes group work, with a focus on creating a safe space for students to share their writing. He argues that professional writers understand something essential about their process that many teachers do not—that writing is a gift. He clarifies this distinction by explaining that the basic human act of giving carries no expectation of receiving something in return:

> Writers are more apt to understand writing as giving: "Here. Take it. Enjoy it. Thank me. (Pay me, if possible). But I'm not interested right now in evaluation or criticism." Many teachers, on the other hand, usually can't think of anything to do with a set of words except to formulate criticism of one sort or the other. (Elbow, 1973, p. 21)

Regie Routman, author of *Writing Essentials*, is another advocate for shared writing. She observes that sharing provides invaluable opportunities for modeling—allowing students to witness and emulate peers who may be more proficient. Routman emphasizes this is not a one-way process. Rather, it welcomes students from diverse backgrounds to contribute their cultural experiences, languages, and literacies to the group at large. She adds, "Receiving validation for their ideas in front of their peers builds students' confidence, a necessary prerequisite for becoming a writer" (Routman, 2005, p. 85).

Routman and Elbow echo my journalistic learning philosophy. Writing should be a collaborative effort that is a shared experience. The examples cited illustrate how easy it is to introduce information-based texts such as newspapers and magazines into a language arts curriculum with very little expense.

As students move into writing their own stories, they continue the practice of reading their stories aloud. Paired sharing provides opportunities for students to hear which portions of their writing excel and which others may sound off the mark. Peer editing encourages students to step outside the confines of their self-interests and to invest in the success of classmates. It also enhances listening skills.

Craig Bark's classroom experiences exemplify the potential of these strategies. Before being hired as an ELA teacher at Palo Alto High School, Bark taught for 17 years in Paramount, California, where there were a higher number of students with learning challenges. Getting through a week in Paramount was often contingent on how effective administrators were at separating rival gangs.

Bark said that students who demonstrated academic prowess at Paramount risked being ostracized by some of the tougher students, who were mostly embarrassed that peers might discover their inability to read and write. He reflected on how certain students intimidated others. "You did not want to be called a 'school boy' in certain neighborhoods because that was how you would get beaten up," Bark said.

Yet Bark developed a reputation for being able to connect and produce results with the more difficult students whom others had written off. In the spirit of Paulo Freire, he established a bond with his students built on trust—and softened several of the hardest class members who were thought to be unreachable.

Bark noted several highly relevant issues that make his former and present work experiences worlds apart:

1. Relevance/Meaning. Bark noted that it was not that his former students could not learn. Rather, they were not being engaged in a manner that showed them that school was relevant. Many came from families that were doing their best just to get by. What many might consider to be great works of literature were not presented to students in ways that were in sync with their everyday concerns.

TECHNOLOGY TIP

With appropriate direction, the Internet is an invaluable resource for accessing wide varieties of educational media. Ask students to note the differences between printed and electronically broadcast stories. Encourage experimentation with audio and video. Radio stories are crafted for the ear and are often embellished with natural sounds that provide audiences with a sense of place. Video adds yet another dimension that can captivate viewers. The ubiquitous availability of smartphones and, increasingly, tablet devices, provides new avenues for learning. Students can gather images, sounds, and video, mixing media to tell stories in inventive ways. However, writing remains a foundational skill that provides structure for other expressions of media. Great movies rely on a good script, and the most effective videos and photos have a narrative arc.

Radio and television sources, such as NPR and CNN, can be invaluable. Play back several examples of broadcast news stories in class. "This American Life," the popular public radio program hosted by Ira Glass, offers great examples of nonfiction storytelling that employ a wide variety of literary devices found in fiction. They include surprise, suspense, and use of dramatic tension. Engage students in a discussion about differences in approach and style.

Critical thinking involves researching several perspectives, weighing evidence, and drawing conclusions. However, assessing the validity of information is not always easy. Have students research and weigh the evidence reported in the incidents that led to the suspension of NBC news anchor Brian Williams. Historically, an anchorperson seated behind a desk was associated with objective storytelling, but not anymore, since the proliferation of 24-hour news networks. Opinion-based programs tend to dominate prime time on news channels because they garner higher ratings than straight news.

Challenge students to compare a variety of media, in the way Wojcicki has her students compare written stories. Does the brevity offered by broadcast stories come at the expense of depth? Do some media outlets appear to be more favorable to certain perspectives?

Engage students further by experimenting with audio and video storytelling. Such exercises allow students to learn how pictures and words can work together to provide context and clarity. Encourage open sharing of the works and critical discussions about the assignments' effectiveness. Ease any concerns about your own knowledge gap by inviting professionals to speak with your class. Skype, iChat,

and Google Hangouts are invaluable resources for extending learning beyond the walls of your classroom.

2. Pedagogical Approach. Much like Freire, Bark showed his Paramount
    students they were not deficient or unable to learn. He discovered
    they knew more than they believed. Bark initiated a practice of
    having students bring two copies of their written assignments to
    class, one of which they would hand to a peer. Students would read
    their assigned partner's paper aloud, while the author listened and
    made notations with a highlight marker. Bark discovered that his
    students could hear when sentences sounded awkward or when the
    grammar was off the mark. Through these paired learning exercises,
    students were able to correct many of the papers' egregious errors
    before they reached his desk. It is an approach he still uses with his
    ELA students at Palo Alto High School.

Bark's approach is consistent with the social learning theories and
practice examined throughout this book (Lave & Wenger, 1991; Vygotsky, 1987; Wenger, 1998), which include collaborative work and scaffolding students who stand to benefit from additional support. In the
same way that Wojcicki has her freshmen students read and dissect newspaper articles aloud, something appears to resonate with students who
have a chance to hear their own words.

Journalism was an unfamiliar discipline for Bark. However, coming to
Palo Alto High, where it is engrained the culture, allowed him to witness
its positive influence on students:

They're interested because they can speak about things that are interesting to them. They do articles about their friends, about issues in
their lives—issues in their community. They're putting it out there for
people to read, and they're getting feedback . . . as opposed to just
doing an analysis of a 400-year-old story.

My final question for Bark was whether he thought journalistic learning strategies would make a difference for his former Paramount students:

Regardless of the school, I think if we could bring writing into the
classroom, where they can learn a structure and use it to express ideas,
and use it to find some value in what they did—and get some feedback from what 'I've' created—that might be something that could
draw them into doing more writing. But, how do you evaluate that
to the state standards and tests? That's the disconnect.

Bark raised another salient issue that impacts the ability of educators to provide students the benefits of journalistic learning strategies. A common policy of "social promotion" advances students who have not demonstrated proficiency at essential skills in grade school to higher grade levels. By the time students at Paramount reached Bark's high school classroom, many were so far behind in language arts that they were required to take two or three remedial courses. These were makeup classes that might otherwise allow space in their schedules for courses like journalism that are classified as electives. In contrast, most of the students he encounters at Palo Alto High School are working ahead of grade level. In fact, he admits that many challenge him. Electives at schools like Palo Alto High School allow students to explore new genres of reading, writing, and learning.

Bark's observations raise questions about the efficacy of repeated attempts to engage challenged learners through traditional methods that do not speak to their intrinsic interests or immediate concerns. Eurocentric and historically oriented texts and writing assignments can seem irrelevant to students who may be dealing with domestic struggles and instability at home. As Bark suggests, journalism can provide these students with a tangible outlet for exploring their challenges while improving their skills. His insights are beneficial to teachers who may never share his experience working in social settings that are so dramatically distinct.

REFLECTIONS ON RELEVANCE

The notion that students are more likely to want to write about themes that are relevant to their lived experiences seems commonsensical. Yet such assignments are not commonplace in secondary education. This is not to negate the value of writing assignments that relate to classic literature and other fiction. Rather, it is a strategy that can strike a balance and introduce students to the forms of informational texts they are more likely to encounter in college, in careers, and in life. An initial focus on relevant topics meets students "where they are" in terms of interests and aptitude. Having engaged them in writing about intrinsic interests, you'll find it easier to move on to other challenging texts.

TAKEAWAYS

Newspapers and magazines are an excellent resource.

- Older editions of publications are abundantly available and essentially free.

- Paired sharing and reading aloud develops listening and peer editing skills.
- Have students distinguish between news stories and opinion articles.
- Encourage X-ray reading for form rather than content.

Explore a variety of nonfiction genres.

- Have students write autobiographical articles, profiles, reviews, and op-eds.
- Pair stronger writers with students who need support.
- Encourage students to experiment with free writing to loosen inhibitions.

Embrace technology.

- Experiment with free platforms including Google Docs, Tumblr, and WordPress.
- Incorporate materials from credible media sources, including NPR and CNN.
- Have students critically examine all sources for transparency and accuracy.

RESOURCES

Watch Esther Wojcicki speak about pedagogical practices at Palo Alto High School: http://ow.ly/ox45D

CNN Student News – Educator and Parent Guides: www.cnn.com/2011/11/10/studentnews/parent-educator-guides/

Columbia Scholastic Press Association: cspa.columbia.edu

Intensive Journalistic Writing Institute: ijwi.net

Journalism Education Association Online Resources: jea.org

New York Times Newspaper in Education online guides: www.nytimes.com/learning/teachers/NIE/

Washington Post Newspaper in Education online guides: nie.washingtonpost.com

Writing News Leads

Purdue University Online Writing Lab: owl.english.purdue.edu/owl/resource/735/05/

CubReporters.org: cubreporters.org/leads.html

Poynter Institute:www.poynter.org/news/media-innovation/11745/the-power-of-leads/

CHAPTER THREE

Discovery
Exploring and Interpreting Information

> "My feeling about WikiLeaks is that we should only publish information if it has some meaning," Amanda asserts in a spirited small group exchange with her high school classmate Jordan. "It's not our job to look into the future." He responds, "Exactly. It's not our job to screen what's worth reporting . . . I'm playing devil's advocate."

As the WikiLeaks story unfolded in 2010, Palo Alto High School students engaged in lively debates about national security and the public's right to access sensitive information. Instructor Paul Kandell's students explore current events and ethical dilemmas on a regular basis, often by imagining how they might act if faced with such issues. Kandell's classroom is a visual archive of historic moments in time. Dozens of memorable editions of *Time* and *Newsweek* hang from the ceiling like floating Christmas ornaments.

At first glance, this might seem like a civics class. However, its objectives are firmly grounded in English language arts. In this course students follow current events and publish the Paly Voice, an online site that reports campus news and feature stories. It provides journalistic learning insights that can be applied in any ELA classroom, regardless of whether the intent is to create a student-run news site.

The Common Core asserts that for students to be college- and career-ready, they should spend more time reading and interpreting informational texts than they have traditionally spent exploring fiction. How else will they be prepared to navigate in an increasingly complex world?

The introduction to the Common Core calls for students to "reflexively demonstrate the cogent reasoning and use of evidence that is essential to both private deliberation and responsible citizenship in a democratic republic. In short, students who meet the Standards develop the skills in reading, writing, speaking, and listening that are the foundation for any creative and purposeful expression of language" (CCSS, p. 3).

This chapter explores how major news stories can be integrated into curricula to teach critical thinking, enhance civic engagement, and examine ethical dilemmas. It also provides examples of how to localize topics, making them more relevant to students. Further, the chapter offers strategies for use of primary texts, such as judicial transcripts.

The WikiLeaks case provided a perfect teachable moment because it touched on delicate matters of national security versus government transparency—and there were any number of perspectives to speak from. How much should the public be entitled to know about the affairs of government? Does transparency potentially come with a cost?

Through the discussion of these matters, students discover nuances about the use and power of language. The descriptive nature of journalism requires that reporters and their editors make linguistic choices. Despite all attempts at objectivity, words convey meaning and can frame a story. And certain words carry a charge. Is Julian Assange, the main figure behind WikiLeaks, an activist or a journalist? Is Edward Snowden, the exiled computer specialist who disclosed classified secrets, a whistle-blower or a traitor? How might a writer's choice of words shape public perceptions? And, how might those perceptions change over time? Snowden was nominated for a Nobel Peace Prize. However, historians often provide the definitive narrative that prevails.

The discovery process for Kandell's students begins at home. Before class, he asks that they read up on the assigned topics, watch newscasts, and listen to radio coverage. Students learn to make distinctions by comparing media interpretations to their own.

Inviting classroom discussion is not a new pedagogical strategy. It is a standard practice in most classrooms. However, often it stops at the level of third-person observation. Teachers engage their students in *talking about* events rather than *talking as though* they are active participants—with something at stake in the outcome. Kandell asks his students to shift their orientation from student observers to active journalists. After making sure they understand the "watchdog" mission of the press, he asks that they weigh the issues at hand as though their words and actions will make a difference. They must consider the responsibilities that come with the power to publish to a mainstream audience.

News stories like WikiLeaks that report on ethical issues challenge students to read and write critically about complex subjects. Students discover that public opinion can shift as more information is revealed. In this context, journalism facilitates and furthers public discussion about how a society governs and responds to matters of ethics. We want privacy and security, but to what degree are we willing to trade one for the other?

DISCUSSION TIPS:
DISCOVERY THROUGH LOCALIZING ETHICAL DILEMMAS

Jordan's group turns to the topic of medical records. In a hypothetical example cited, a student newspaper has been leaked documents revealing potentially damaging information about a school board member who has a serious health condition. Jordan and his team must envision themselves as the publication's editorial board and decide whether to go public with the story. "WikiLeaks is one thing," Shelby says, "but publishing someone's medical records just because you have access to them isn't right."

"But public figures should be held to a different level of accountability than you or me," Jordan counters. "We have an expectation of privacy."

Amanda rejects Jordan's argument and asserts, "School board members are not public figures."

Melissa adds, "If it [his condition] doesn't interfere with how he does his job . . . then it doesn't make a difference. It doesn't mean [imply] any kind of scandal or scheme." As their discussion concludes, they agree to disagree.

As leader, Kelsey asks each group to provide the class with a short synopsis of their discussion points. Most discovered that determining what constitutes legitimate news is not always easy. Several students noted that editorial policies could depend on a publication's tone and intended audience. In other words, what is appropriate for *People* magazine may not be appropriate for *Time* magazine.

From the back of the room, Kandell suggests a new scenario. "Do you encourage hacking?" he asks. "Let's say Sean's friend is the hacker and says, 'I'll convey the information to you. Protect me, and I'll go out and get you lots more [information].'"

Dillon, another class member, counters, "Our argument would be that we're actually inspiring better security. By revealing that their information can be hacked they will spend more money to protect it." Students chuckle.

Kandell sarcastically questions whether banks would buy that argument. "Hey, it's not my fault. Make your security better. I'm walking away," Kandell says. The room erupts in laughter.

In a third scenario, the groups are to imagine they have received leaked documents revealing how Palo Alto High School's standardized test scores rank compared to other area high schools.

Jordan is adamant: "This is public information that will eventually be revealed, and it's not damaging to anyone. It's not revealing information about individual students."

Amanda agrees. "If it's newsworthy—damaging or not—it should be published."

From across the room, Marlie counters, "The numbers are going to be the same two weeks later, when they are [officially] released."

"No, we are breaking news," Amanda asserts.

"It will be just as 'breaking' two weeks later," Marlie says. Kelsey, in her role as class leader, lets that be the final word.

Having students lead class discussions of this nature is one of Kandell's key strategies. "My students are more responsive to their peers than they would be to me," he says. "Why not give them that leadership opportunity?" Not only do his students lead discussions, but Kandell relies on them to choose the topics. Students respond positively to having a voice and a role in every step of the process. Kandell is an award-winning journalism teacher who uses the same strategies in his other English classes. He shared:

It's the same thing in my English classes as in my journalism classes—get the students up in front of the room. I train students how to ask questions, and how to be leaders, and then they are in charge of the class. We'll go through a chapter of a book, with students taking the lead. If I had to be the one who designed every class and was always in front of the room, it would be exhausting for me. I wouldn't be able to do it and they'd get sick of me.

Michelle Balmeo agrees. She also seeks to make her English classes more like her journalism classes by enlisting high-performing students to serve as mentors. Much like student publication editors, these students are called writing coaches and serve as role models and leaders:

If you ask anyone who teaches both they will say that it is such a success for English because kids in English see English as such a disconnected thing that they are uninvested in, and kids in journalism are completely invested. So much of the work you would do in an English class the kids do with each other in a journalism class.

Balmeo collaborated with history teachers at her school to create an interdisciplinary project-based course called American Studies. During fall term, students look at the topic of immigration and migration through various literary forms, including fiction, nonfiction, and poetry. Student teams must approach the subject from a specific angle, such as how immigrant populations confront issues related to education, healthcare, or assimilation. They select an immigrant to interview, and they write a profile story with photos that is later published. Balmeo identifies and grooms prospective student writing coaches from year one. They are mentored and are prepared by senior year to become mentors. Writing coaches peer review student work before it reaches Balmeo's desk. "The first year they are being trained, and then every year after they are expected to do the trainings, which in turn makes them better writers."

Training mostly centers on giving students opportunities to practice. The leadership team often meets after class to engage in mock run-throughs. Simulating new and potentially stress-producing activities often calls up the same anxieties one would experience in the actual situation. Yet these practice sessions provide students with a safe space to experiment and grow.

Sharing control of a class with students requires trust—in one's students and in oneself. Losing control of a class, or being at a loss for an answer, are two common concerns —especially of inexperienced teachers.

However, part of this fear is grounded in an obsolete paradigm of what it means to teach. It is the false belief that teachers should be infallible experts. A solution is to set a collaborative tone for your class from day one. Acknowledge that you do not and will not have all the answers. Make it clear that the course is about teachers and students "rolling up their sleeves" and exploring together.

Journalistic learning asserts that questions can be more powerful than answers. Answers often lead to finite conclusions. Powerful questions lead to ongoing discovery.

Discussion allows participants to test and sharpen their rhetorical skills. Discussion leaders learn to moderate exchanges between peers, with an eye on keeping them fair and accurate. This give and take provides students with opportunities to experience democracy in action. The process gives a richer sense of understanding, in line with the tenets of the Common Core.

What is clear from observation is that Kandell's students are authentically engaged in learning, but why? His students are not passively reading and writing about the events of the day. Kandell is not asking his students to memorize facts or fill in worksheets that simulate the experience of a standardized test. Metaphorically, they are stepping into the shoes of the central players in the case and envisioning the actions they might take given the circumstances.

The discovery process brought the issue closer to home when class discussion turned to the issue of censorship on PalyVoice.com, the news site published by the class. At issue was whether editors should review reader comments before posting them publicly. Jordan, who had engaged in the WikiLeaks debate, also argued for trusting students to act appropriately when posting comments: "I just think that if someone has something to say, they should be allowed to say it. That is the good thing about our country. The discussion should be allowed to proceed unless there is a problem. I'm in favor of them censoring it afterward, if it is inflammatory."

It was ultimately decided that editors should review comments prior to publication but not alter the content of those comments. Comments containing inflammatory language were omitted.

DISCOVERY THROUGH COMPLEX TEXTS

Colleen Simpson is another ELA educator who relies heavily on journalistic learning principles and strategies. She teaches Advanced Placement

---

COMMON CORE STRATEGIES

The expectation is that college- and career-ready students will proficiently do the following:

- Work with peers to promote civil, fair, and decisive discussions; set clear goals, deadlines, and roles.
- Drive conversations by posing and responding to questions that probe reasoning and evidence; weigh a full range of positions; clarify, verify, and challenge ideas and assumptions; resolve contradictions; promote contrasting and original perspectives.
- Acknowledge diverse perspectives; synthesize comments, claims, and evidence from all sides; resolve contradictions; conduct deeper research.

These standards relate to effective leadership. To empower leaders, provide skill-building opportunities. Set specific times for training and development. Take the initial lead and provide clear guidelines. Acknowledge the fact that student leaders can expect unforeseen challenges when managing peers. Fairness and transparency are essential. Student leaders need to understand that they are not "teachers" in the traditional sense of the term. Matters relating to grades and discipline are not their responsibility. Appropriateness is essential, and matters of confidentiality must be observed.

From this point on, allow the team to drive the process—with teacher advisement. Student leaders need to know they can (and should) consult their teacher if matters get murky. In-class instruction led by student team members can lead to higher levels of student engagement. Removing the conventional "top-down" style of class management in this manner can be an essential factor. It can help to bridge a generational gap that commonly exists between teachers and students, keeping course content fresh and relevant.

Hold new elections, according to pre-established intervals, to allow other students to experience the benefits of leadership. These are life skills that better prepare students for college and careers.

English Language and Composition, College Prep American Literature, and Honors English in Plymouth County, Massachusetts. The discovery process for her students begins with assigning selected essays from the *New Yorker* and *Atlantic Monthly* that focus on deep observation. One chronicles the intricacies of the seemingly mundane experiences of late-night shoppers at a CVS/pharmacy. Another explores the interactions between tailgaters at an Ole Miss football game. She specifically selects articles offering rich descriptive details to inspire students to strengthen their own observation skills.

Simpson has her students engage in local 3–4-hour excursions where they are challenged to take notes on the minutia that fills everyday life in their own community. Small details expose students to a rich tapestry of illuminating experiences. The fieldwork experiences provide material for original essays her students may have never imagined writing before.

Simpson introduces additional rhetorical modes as the academic year progresses. She wants her students to make distinctions about sections of text that compare and contrast, are descriptive, or that categorize—to name a few. To illustrate, she asks students to follow a columnist of their choice for an extended period. Having a say in selecting a writer motivates students to authentically commit to the assignment. Some choose columnists who write about news and politics, whereas others may follow sports or lifestyle writers.

Students are asked to read at least 10 examples of a writer's work. Digging deeper, students learn to identify rhetorical devices employed by the columnist, such as use of alliteration, irony, or metaphors. This approach ties directly to the Common Core's emphasis on close reading, discussed in Chapter 2.

Simpson also assigns texts that explore nonfiction-writing conventions, including *On Writing Well*, by William Zinsser, and *Thank You For Arguing*, by Jay Heinrichs. The books provide a foundation for more critical close readings of complex texts. Students explore logical fallacies in writing to better understand distinctions in ethos, logos, and pathos.

Another assignment Simpson gives is to emulate their chosen writer's style in a column of their own. Students discover the power of word use, sentence structure, effective flow, and appropriate tone. In time, they are able to identify and replicate strategies that give rise to an author's distinctive "voice." With these insights, students next tackle writing their own columns. The emphasis is on more complex use of rhetorical devices to engage readers. Students gain more confidence in establishing a narrative arc. Problems expressed in narratives emerge as challenges for resolution and opportunities for personal growth.

Similar strategies are proving to be effective at a high school in Delaware, Ohio. Julienne McClain's 11th- and 12th-grade students were considered perpetual poor performers. "Our school was struggling a couple of years ago with students not being engaged. We had huge truancy problems and epic failures because kids didn't know how to work, and

---

COMMON CORE STRATEGIES

Observation assignments are directly tied to Common Core's emphasis on research. Proficient students are expected to do the following:

- Engage in short-term and long-term research projects that answer a given or self-generated question; limit or expand investigation when appropriate; synthesize multiple sources, and demonstrate comprehension.
- Use descriptive words and phrases to convey vivid images.
- Provide a conclusion that reflects on what is experienced, observed, or resolved in the narrative.

Observation exercises can be as simple as observing a dog or cat's behavior in great detail for an extended period of time. Encourage students to increase their repertoire of descriptive words and phrases to add texture to their writing. An otherwise mundane experience can be expressed imaginatively. Rather than stating, "The cat walked across the room," one could say, "The cat slinked forward pensively." Rather than "The dog rested on the floor," how about "The dog lounged in the corner, oblivious to passersby."

---

didn't want to work," McClain said. However, she was committed to making a difference.

McClain made her principal several bold promises. She pledged to deliver higher test scores than the school's average on state exams, lower truancy problems, engage students, and make better writers. However, the promises came with a catch. She refused to teach fiction. McClain does not abhor novels or prose. Her intention was to counterbalance the vast amounts of fiction she trusted students were exposed to in their other English classes.

Like Simpson, McClain encourages her students to discover the wonders of writing through reading well-written works—and specifically good journalism. She has found that fact-based stories seem to resonate with her students in profound ways. They find nonfiction and journalistic works to be more relevant to their own experiences.

She teams strong students with classmates who are struggling. McClain also invites students to collaborate with her in developing course assignments. Like Kandell and Simpson, she finds students commit at higher levels when they have a say in crafting their assignments.

One project involves having student teams identify and profile famous journalists. Previous choices have included Nellie Bly and Hunter

S. Thompson. McClain introduces argument persuasion and the distinctions between logos, ethos, and pathos. Students are challenged to identify examples of those concepts in their chosen journalist's works. After researching and writing profiles, the teams make a formal front-of-the-room presentation of their findings to the class. The presentations include Microsoft PowerPoint slides and often the use of audiovisual elements.

McClain's students read U.S. Supreme Court transcripts from *Tinker vs. Des Moines*, a landmark decision that more broadly defined constitutionally protected free speech. Mary Beth Tinker was suspended from school in 1965 for wearing a black armband in protest of U.S. involvement in the Vietnam War. The Court ruled that the Des Moines Independent School District erred in punishing her for expressing her First Amendment rights.

Journalists often have to pore over dense documents and summarize their meaning for a broader audience. Deep research of primary sources

---

COMMON CORE STRATEGIES

The Common Core asks that teachers draw on seminal documents to have students become proficient at the following:

- Discovering and analyzing original U.S. texts, including application of constitutional principles and use of legal reasoning (for example, U.S. Supreme Court majority opinions and dissents).
- Examining primary U.S. documents of historical and literary significance, including how they address related themes and concepts.

Introduce the concept of working with primary informational texts by having students examine local historical records. Have them conduct an online search for your state or city's founding documents. If Internet access is limited, invite local archivists or historians as guests and ask that they bring samples of historical papers and other artifacts.

Engage students in a discussion about how many cultures have no remaining records that document their origin. For some cultures, traditions called for the passing down of oral histories. Others have lost their historical documents to disasters, wars, or genocide. Honest discussion about the marginalization and oppression of various populations helps students from all backgrounds place themselves and their families within a broader historical context and allows them to value their origins—with or without access to primary sources.

allows McClain's students to understand how the Court's decision affects their own rights to freedom of self-expression—a freedom they might otherwise take for granted. Team assignments of this nature give students opportunities to mentor one another and to collectively take their skills to new levels.

McClain implemented a strategy that relied heavily on discovery through journalistic practices—and delivered on her promise that first year. Ninety-seven percent of her sophomore students passed the Ohio State reading and writing exams, compared to her school's average passing rate of 87 percent.

EXPLORING OBJECTIVITY AND OPINION

Writing about what was read and discussed is the next step in journalistic learning. Effective writing demonstrates comprehension and an ability to formulate ideas in an organized way. Journalists are often tasked with breaking down complex topics in a manner that can easily be understood. For example, matters of science can be riddled with jargon that is only understood by experts in the field. Journalistic writing seeks to provide readers and audience with the essential facts.

However, distinguishing facts from fiction is not always easy. Often the "facts" are contested—even among experts. For decades, humanity's role in climate change was heavily debated. However, mounting evidence has all but silenced the most outspoken detractors. Effective writers learn to present opposing views and acknowledge which are considered credible, given the current understanding in a field of expertise. Journalists seek first-person accounts and verifiable data. They present the facts and allow readers and audiences to form an opinion.

Of course, whether journalists can ever be authentically objective is also a contested topic. Everyone brings some perspective to the work that he or she does. A growing consensus of media professionals acknowledges this truth. Objectivity is an aspiration rather than an absolute. Opinions have their place, and it is generally not considered to be on the front page of a newspaper, news site, or a factual course assignment. A news journalist's job is to report, not take a position.

The same is true when writing other information-oriented texts. Researchers and analysts in a business setting use the same skills. When a company is faced with making a critical decision, it relies on workers who can make an accurate assessment of the circumstances that delves beneath surface assumptions.

Yet there are venues where advocacy is welcome and persuasive writing is appropriate. In media, commentaries and opinion pieces complement news writing in many publications. They can provide readers with context, analysis, and perspective. In all instances, writers of information-based texts should be transparent about their practices—disclosing conflicts of interests or biases as they arise.

Likewise, in business and science, writers are called upon to provide an opinion—to draw informed conclusions from data. Decisions must be made about the next course of action with any project. Do present results warrant a continued investment of money, time, and other resources?

It is not uncommon for writers to alter their opinion about a subject when faced with new information or after sufficient time for reflection. Journalistic work is about the uncompromising search for truth, and noble pursuits require effort. Students learn not to accept any single source at face value. Media may inform their opinions, but ultimately young adults must learn to think for themselves.

Ellen Austin also encourages her students to deeply analyze informational texts for clarity and ambiguity and to think for themselves. While teaching English and journalism at Palo Alto High School, her students sometimes encountered ethical dilemmas that had them weigh personal interests against serving the greater good. Erik is a Palo Alto senior who wrote a commentary in class for the school's online publication that caused a stir with executives at Common Applications. The company is an online service utilized by many universities to centralize submissions of college admissions applications. Erik discovered and reported about technical flaws in the system's software:

> The story was called "Rejecting the Common App." I found that it had a lot of technical glitches, like cutting off half of your text. I submitted an application, but when I clicked "submit," it inconspicuously sliced off one of my paragraphs, even though the essay was within the specified word-count limitations.

A few weeks after Erik's article appeared, one of the school's career counselors sent him an email that included a message from the Common Application's CEO, accusing him of reporting erroneous untruths. The school's counselor advised Erik and publication editors to remove the post.

Austin, the course instructor and publication adviser, reminded her students that the company's charges carried the prospect of severe implications. Publishing false statements is potentially libelous. Megan, one of the online publication's student editors, recalled:

We weren't really sure what to do—but we sent back a cordial response, asking for specific instances where the article was in error. We never got a response, so we left it up. The stakes were high because many of this organization's board members are potentially heads of colleges that could be reviewing our own applications at some point.

Erik noted that the *New York Times* reported a similar story about the Common Application several months after his. Megan shared that the eventual outcome was bittersweet:

Ironically, a few weeks later, the Common Applications site posted a notice informing users that there is a 150-character limit.

Erik cited how his own experience using the Common App contradicted its instructions and its company's claims. Speaking truth to power is a fundamental practice of journalism professionals. It requires steadfast courage in times of uncertainty. Erik, his editors, and their advisers engaged in numerous internal discussions regarding the most appropriate courses of action. However, instructor guidance is critical for grounding such learning activities. Instructors mentor their students through these exchanges by supporting rather than steering their deliberations about ethical issues.

The Common Core State Standards that relate to writing informative texts call for students in grade 11 and 12 to not only cite evidence, but to tackle ambiguity, conflicting ideas, and complexity.

INSTITUTIONAL CHALLENGES

Kandell, Balmeo, Simpson, and McClain are motivating their students to think by making bold curricular changes that are not always welcome. Journalistic learning strategies can challenge the status quo by engaging students in current events with controversial themes and unpredictable outcomes. They steer teaching away from reliance on standardized textbooks, test-based worksheets, and memorization exercises. Introducing these strategies can be unsettling in school cultures with administrators who do not welcome autonomy or support nontraditional practices.

Teachers who seek to innovate can feel restricted by structures that were designed for an industrial age that has long since passed. Schools primarily provide youths with a state-mandated institutional experience, which occurs within the confines of four walls, during prescribed hours,

---

COMMON CORE STRATEGIES

College- and career-ready high school graduates are expected to competently do the following:

- Cite credible evidence to support analysis of texts, whether they are explicit, inferred, or ambiguous.
- Identify two or more main ideas of a text, analyze their development, and provide an objective summary.
- Analyze a complex set of ideas or events, and explain the interactions between people, ideas, or events as they unfold.

To build upon these skills, have students break into small groups and take turns reflecting about times they may have faced an ethical dilemma. The persons sharing should articulate both sides of the argument, and describe the decision ultimately reached and the rationale that informed the decision. Would he or she take the same course of action if faced with a similar situation today? What did he or she learn from the experience?

---

and that is structured by specific protocols. Students not only attend schools, they are *schooled*—a process of socialization that purports to prepare them for higher levels of education, gainful employment, civic engagement, and fulfilling lives (Kosar, 2011).

Pedagogical practice largely centers on the one-way dissemination of knowledge, from a single teacher to a class of students, who are theorized to be receptors of that knowledge. Student roles within this dominant paradigm are understandably passive and predictable. In many communities this model is challenged by ever increasing class sizes due to budget shortfalls and teacher layoffs (Ravitch, 2010).

The structural design of schools and learning spaces is also a factor. The physical layout of classrooms remains greatly unchanged since their inception (Cuban, 1993). Typically, rows of desks face forward, forming an audience for a sole instructor who directs learning (Oakes & Lipton, 2007). Most often, teacher-guided instruction follows a lesson plan, which designates curricular objectives and measures, with great specificity. Students are socialized to raise a hand to signal they can provide their teacher with anticipated "right" answers. They are also expected to assimilate what they learn, and in turn demonstrate prescribed proficiencies.

This type of socialization can diminish creativity among students in the classroom. Ron Beghetto, a prominent education and social psychology professor at University of Connecticut who researches and writes on creativity in the classroom, speaks of what some of his colleagues refer to as "the tyranny of the lesson plan." Elaborating further, Beghetto notes that "teachers often plan creativity out of their classrooms by following plans that are excessively structured." He references a pervasive pattern of classroom talk called the "IRE pattern" (Mehan, 1979); IRE is an acronym for Initiate, Respond, and Evaluate. Students quickly learn that their role is to wait for the teacher to pose a question, to raise a hand in response, to provide the expected answer, and then wait for validation. Beghetto argues that this staid approach to teaching is inadequate in an age that is defined by an increasing sense of ambiguity and complexity in the world. It also leaves little room for spontaneity and bursts of rich, free-flowing interactions between teachers and students, as well as between students and their peers, which can create transformative learning experiences.

Beghetto notes that there is a disparity between how curricula are planned and how they are ultimately executed. Tension occurs when, out of habit, teachers attempt to subject the natural unfolding that occurs to the confines of the plan. Strictly sticking to the plan undermines a teacher's desire to stimulate creativity in a classroom. Simultaneously, disregarding the plan, and the sole pursuit of spontaneity, often creates a fear of curricular chaos. The result is a paradox. Beghetto explains that there is an "in-between space" where creativity and planning can coexist.

He posits that this space is where "micromoments" can be discovered. Micromoments are

> fleeting, easy-to-miss classroom interactions and experiences (e.g., a student stumbles forth an idea and the teacher nods reassuringly for her to continue; a hand is raised, but the student is not called on). Many of these moments are, in the big picture of schooling, easily overlooked and may seem to have little lasting effect on students. However, repeated negative experiences during these micromoments can accrue over time and have a profound impact. (Beghetto, 2009, p. 2)

Inviting students to experience micromoments through peer-led interaction adds yet another dimension to learning that follows the journalistic model. In a typical newsroom setting, reporters compete and advance based on their effectiveness in story pitch sessions. Successful reporters learn to advocate for themselves and their ideas. An editor who guides this process develops a discerning ear. He or she cultivates an acute ability to listen as a steward, concerned with accuracy, fairness, and publishing for the sake of the public good.

Having an opportunity to simulate this process empowers students to know their thoughts and that opinions matter. They are no longer bystanders without a stake in the public debate about these issues of grave concern. As such, many have been moved to write their representatives, author letters to local news editors, and publish their work in larger forums. When young people feel unheard, their sense of self suffers (Cummins, 2001).

The results are troubling. More than 7,000 American teens drop out of school every day (a whopping 1.2 million annually), costing our country billions in lost wages (Alliance for Excellent Education, 2012). In a survey of high school dropouts funded by the Bill and Melinda Gates Foundation, 47% cited "boredom" as one of their primary reasons for leaving (Bridgeland, 2006). These trends affect students of color in disproportionate numbers. African American and Hispanic students are less likely than White students to graduate from high school, acquire a college or advanced degree, or earn a middle-class living (NAEP, 2011). Students with diverse and socioeconomically challenged backgrounds are often falsely presumed to have real and unalterable deficits that impede their ability to learn (Ladson-Billings, 1994; Pearl & Knight, 1999). Morrell (2004) counterargues that these students bring a wealth of local knowledge and cultural literacies into classrooms, which are undervalued within a narrow and yet dominant definition of what counts as scholarship. However, in a now classic study of minority students, respondents revealed that "too often the instruction they receive convinces them that what they have to say is irrelevant or wrong" (Cummins, 2001).

Kandell, Simpson, Balmeo, and McClain's students are not bored. These teachers work to make their classrooms a safe space where all perspectives are valued. They tap into what motivates students to excel.

As addressed previously, psychology researchers assert that motivation exists on a continuum. Extrinsic motivations, at lower levels of the scale, include the desire to get good grades, please one's parents, or fulfill one's ego. Intrinsic motivation, at the highest level, is not tied to external reasons. It is said to be catalyzed internally—for the joy of the experience (Deci & Ryan, 1985, 2000). Autonomy, the sense that one is directing his or her actions, is a key component of intrinsic motivation. Taking on leadership roles in class helps students to cultivate autonomy, which also strengthens self-confidence. These skills are essential when the matters at hand require critical thinking.

TECHNOLOGY TIP

Diaries and personal letters are other forms of primary source materials that enrich student learning. Introduce and discuss classics like *The Diary of Anne Frank* or *Twelve Years a Slave* (which chronicles Solomon Northrup's experience of being held in captivity). Show age-appropriate scenes from film depictions of these stories.

Have students document their autobiographies through experimentation with video and/or audio recording. They can incorporate images from family photos and maps. Encourage stories that reflect on some obstacle that was overcome. See resources listed at end of this chapter.

REFLECTIONS ON DISCOVERY

Leadership skills are essential for students to become successful in navigating the complexities of adult life. One specific interaction I witnessed at Palo Alto High School represents how to best engage students in the discovery process. One of Paul Kandell's students approached him to suggest that the school should purchase a certain brand of digital camera for student use. Many teachers would consider the suggestion and make the choice themselves. Instead, Kandell advised her to do further research and comparison—and to construct an evidenced-based argument to present to a committee of student editors who would then make the final decision. She was successful in persuading peers to go with her recommendation. This teachable moment placed responsibility for learning in the hands of the student. Such exercises can be defining moments for young people, challenging them to experience real-world benefits from critical thinking.

TAKEAWAYS

Enliven class discussions by empowering student leaders.

- Foster ownership by having students elect a leadership team.
- Let student leaders choose topics and manage discussions.
- Explore the power of questions rather than answers.

Assign discovery exercises requiring deep observation through fieldwork.

- Seek ideas and inspiration from long-form journalism articles.
- Assign fieldwork and have students take very detailed notes.

Introduce new rhetorical modes of writing.

- Have students write a profile on a famous journalist.
- Have them emulate his or her style.

Incorporate use of primary sources.

- Draw from seminal documents.
- Localize by drawing from city, county, or state archives.
- Acknowledge marginalized communities.

RESOURCES

Online Resources

Searchlights and Sunglasses: Field Notes from the Digital Age of Journalism, by Eric Newton: searchlightsandsunglasses.org

Think Like a Journalist, by Michael Bugeja: newstrust.net/guides

Books

On Writing Well, by William Zinsser

Thank You for Arguing, by Jay Heinrichs

On Writing: A Memoir of the Craft, by Stephen King

Video

Watch Paul Kandell's students debate about WikiLeaks: http://ow.ly/nHxHg

NCTE Rationale for Teaching Challenging Books: www.ncte.org/action/anti-censorship/rationales

Video Diaries: lab.wgbh.org/index.html

Radio Diaries: www.radiodiaries.org

CHAPTER FOUR

Sharing

Personal Stories, Diversity, and Empathy

I'm not just African American. I'm African, Jamaican, and American, so things are different. My sister doesn't believe that she's clearly Black. She believes she's a mixture of things.

—Marcus, Palo Alto High School Junior

Identity classifications are less easily defined than in previous generations. Rather than accept conventional ethnic, racial, and religious labels, 21st-century youth from diverse backgrounds are at liberty to make their own choices about how they self-identify and reject traditional categories by blurring the lines (Rodriguez, 2003). Adolescent years are a critical period in the process of identity formation, as young people endeavor to discover their interests, determine their values, and assert their independence (Hauser, 2011; Leary & Tangney, 2003; Schwartz, Luyckx, & Vignoles, 2011). Schools become social settings where students make declarations about who they are, encounter feedback from peers, and, in turn, mutually influence who they will all become (Carter, 2006; Schwartz, Côté, & Arnett, 2005).

Race, ethnicity, gender, religion, and class are among the many overlapping factors at play in campus settings. Crenshaw (1989) uses the term *intersectionality* to describe a process by which individuals learn to manage their multiple identities. Carter (2006) notes that some students learn to become "culturally flexible," enabling them to navigate between social circles more easily than their co-ethnic peers.

This chapter explores how journalistic learning can contribute to a culture of equity and inclusion in ELA classrooms, creating safe spaces for open dialogue and cultural exchange. Students come to class with unique experiences that deserve to be honored rather than ignored. The chapter looks at writing and media production as outlets for academic growth, self-reflection, and personal empowerment. It addresses the transformative power of journalistic self-expression.

The struggle to define and assert identity is not a new phenomenon. It is a natural rite of passage teens experience in the process of becoming adults. Yet it is manifesting in new ways. The face of America is changing, bringing new significance to the "melting pot" metaphor so often articulated throughout the nation's history. Some contemporary scholars prefer the term "salad bowl" to acknowledge the value of honoring and maintaining cultural distinctions as opposed to full assimilation (Chua, 2007).

The 2010 U.S. Census reported that nearly 36% of the nation's population self-identify as minorities. Non-Hispanic Whites are now the slowest growing group in the United States. Hispanics are the nation's largest minority group (surpassing African Americans), accounting for one-half of the overall U.S. population growth of 27.3 million between 2000 and 2010. In that period, the Hispanic population increased 43% (U.S. Census, 2010).

Other cultural shifts relate to interracial relations. A Pew Research study reveals that interracial marriages have more than doubled, from 6.7% in 1980 to approximately 15% in 2010. Additionally, more than a third of the U.S. population reports having an immediate family member or a close relative who is married to a member of another race (Pew Internet Research, 2012). The number of U.S. citizens who reported being both Black and White has more than doubled since the option was added in 2000, from 785,000 to 1.8 million in 2010 (U.S. Census, 2010).

High school campus life often reflects the dynamics of changes occurring within the broader population. Palo Alto High School's demographic composition and the geographic boundaries that separate its students add to the complexity of peer group interactions. Its historically White student population declined from 73% in 2001 to 53% in 2014 (Ed-Data, 2014). Geographically, the Bayshore freeway divides the city of Palo Alto from the crime-challenged neighboring community of East Palo Alto. Students who reside there are bused to schools in significantly more affluent areas like Palo Alto, and when they arrive generally stay together. It's a scenario that can lead to cultural divides and co-ethnic conflicts.

Marcus and Garrett are twin brothers entering their senior year at Palo Alto High School. Their father immigrated to the United States from Guyana, South America, at age 13, and their mother's parents are Jamaican. Diligence and discipline made it possible for both parents to attend Ivy League–rated Brown University, to pursue professional careers, and to raise their family in the affluent community of Palo Alto. Garrett wears his hair shortly trimmed, whereas Marcus wears dreadlocks. They are an example of how complex identity can be among teenagers, even within a single family. Journalism provides both brothers with a vehicle for reflecting on their choices and expressing their individuality. Yet peer relationships can still be challenging. Garrett acknowledges some of the tensions that can arise:

> I feel like at our school, you still see a lot of racial divides . . . a lot of the students of color come from East Palo Alto. . . . So they just join together immediately after they get off the bus. And there's a place where they all eat lunch. It's really a bonding experience for them. And so, they really have no need to find new friends because they also may have a lot of classes together. And they do a lot of the same sports. So, color sort of unifies them. Personally, I have a lot of Caucasian friends and Hispanic friends. I like to branch out and create a lot of diversity among the people I choose to befriend.

Garrett's statements illustrate the internal struggles students can experience. His challenge is to remain culturally flexible (Carter, 2006) and mindful of the intersections (Crenshaw, 1989) that influence who he will be in multiple spheres. He is a student, with family roots in the United States, Jamaica, and South America living in affluent Palo Alto—and he has also declared himself to be a journalist. He enjoys video work and on-camera reporting. Journalists are trained to step outside of their comfort zones and to question their assumptions. Journalistic-oriented course work has provided both brothers with opportunities to "branch out" and mix with broader groups of students. "I definitely wanted to be a journalist because I took beginning journalism last year as a sophomore, and I was definitely inspired," Garrett said. Both are outspoken on issues that pertain to equity for all students at the high school and view media as effective way to spread ideas and influence opinions.

COUNTERING DIVISIVE STEREOTYPES

Although African Americans have historically been stereotyped as being underachievers (Fischer, 1996; Herrnstein & Murray, 1994), Asian Americans are often characterized as being naturally gifted (Lee, 1994). It is a stereotype that may seem benign, but it can be burdensome for students who feel compelled to meet expectations that they be perfect. The faultless Asian is a familiar trope in popular culture. For example, characters in a third season episode of the successful television series *Glee* joked that an "A–" grade is an "Asian F" (Thompson, 2011).

Sue and Okazaki (1990) found that Asian American students score significantly higher than other groups on three out of six psychological subscales that rate personal concerns about perfectionism. In that study, Asian American students expressed higher depressive symptoms related to concerns about not pleasing their parents, avoiding mistakes, and self-doubt. *The Chronicle of Higher Education* reports that some Asian American students refrain from disclosing their heritage on college entrance applications (Biemiller, 1986). Some fear elite universities may use quota systems to artificially control enrollments (Slotnik, 2012).

With Asian Americans representing 21% of Palo Alto High School's student body (Palo Alto Unified School District, 2012), these dynamics are at play as they work to find themselves and define their identities amid peer and societal pressures. These students can experience significant degrees of internal stress as they attempt to balance their pursuit of intrinsic interests versus their desire to please others (Castro & Rice, 2003). Ill effects can include guilt, depression, and even suicide (Chang, 1998).

Campanile is Palo Alto High School's student newspaper. It is not uncommon to find 60 to 70 "Campi" staffers and editors in one of the school's computer labs as late as 9:30 p.m. on any production weeknight. Rick is Asian American and a section editor. He explains what drives the staff members to stay late, night after night:

> The fact that we're all in it together . . . rather than learning from a single source like the teacher. It's more like we're learning from each other's experiences, which is really awesome because it's really the only time where I've felt like I have had real responsibility. Not just to myself, or to a teacher, or to my parents, but to the newspaper as a whole.

Rick seeks to replace teacher and parental pressures with a more personal, self-determined sense of purpose. He is expressing the strong sense of autonomy and competence he experiences, as well as the sense of relatedness he shares with publication staffers—all consistent with Self-determination Theory (Deci & Ryan, 1985, 2000).

In an earlier interview, Esther Wojcicki addressed why she believes the students demonstrate such a high level of commitment:

> These kids are not going to school to see me, okay. I'm sorry to tell the teachers that. They're coming to school to see their peers, and

it's really important for them to feel like they are connected to their peers. They feel like they're connected to the program, and they're connected to each other.

Relatedness is central in these comments. Fulfillment comes from working in concert with mutually supportive peers. These experiences are not about grades, parents, or teachers.

Rick's demeanor turns solemn when he speaks about the pressures of being Asian American:

> It's just a little irritating. I mean there are definitely some Asian cliques . . . I just chose not to be part of it. I think parents have a lot of influence on that. Like my parents—they're very strict about grades and stuff. But compared to a lot of parents I've seen, they're pretty liberal. But just like this first generation born here—Asian immigrant wave—that creates this huge clique thing. This whole race for college; I definitely feel a hint of disappointment sometimes, just as I'm not like the perfect student.

Rick's comments are consistent with the cited literature, which suggests that Asian American students can experience significant concerns about not meeting parents' expectations (Sue & Okazaki, 1990).

Journalism provides a venue for identity exploration, where Rick can relate to peers outside of restrictive narratives about what it means to be Asian American. For many program participants, being a "journalist" is perceived as a distinct identity—apart from race, ethnicity, and other categories. It can provide a new vantage point from which to critique the dominant narratives that otherwise influence their lives, and the view can be refreshing.

Discussions and writing assignments that get published provide students with constructive ways to air their concerns and facilitate new understanding. However, these issues are not easy. Race and ethnicity are complex and potentially unsettling topics that some teachers would prefer to avoid or believe would be better addressed in social studies classes. Yet opportunities for students to share their thoughts and feelings about these tensions—through talks, readings, and written assignments—offer potential pathways for reaching otherwise hesitant learners (Hess & Posselt, 2002). As discussed in Chapter 2, students often respond to assignments that relate to their lived experiences, and these educational activities are aligned with the Common Core.

The opportunity to write and share about one's experiences may not immediately appeal to every student. For some, knowledge about

---

COMMON CORE STRATEGIES

The introductory section of the Common Core State Standards clearly stresses the curricular value of classwork that pertains to bridging relationships between cultures. It states, to meet the standards for college- and career-readiness:

> Students appreciate that the twenty-first-century classroom and workplace are settings in which people from often widely divergent cultures and who represent diverse experiences and perspectives must learn and work together. Students actively seek to understand other perspectives and cultures through reading and listening and they are able to communicate effectively with people of varied backgrounds (CCSS-ELA, p. 3).

Teachers who remain nervous about guiding students as they explore journalistic writing genres and sensitive topics are likely to ask where to start. Assigning students to interview peers, as discussed in Chapter 2, is a great way to support them in bridging cultural gaps prior to any specific incident that may provoke tension.

To facilitate cultural exchange, have students pair up with classmates they do not know well. Give each pair a set time to interview one another about family traditions and customs. Findings might relate to practices, holidays, or cuisine. Next, have teammates photograph one another and write 350–500 words about what they discovered. Publish or post the completed assignments and discuss the results. Such assignments provide a positive way for students to share customs and traditions that may otherwise be unfamiliar to their peers. Accordingly, such assignments allow students opportunities to begin to value difference rather than fear it.

---

journalism and its practices may be limited. Reasons can be cultural and generational. The arrival of a daily newspaper on a doorstep, enjoyed with a cup of coffee and breakfast, is an iconic but fading image in homes across America. As media continue to migrate online, students are less likely to be raised in households where following the news, via the Internet or traditional print sources, is modeled by parents or guardians (Kohut, 2013). This can lead some students to disregard the educational and civic value many associate with being informed about current events, and to assume that mainstream press coverage is "not for them." Such beliefs can be aggravated when news organizations commit limited resources to reporting on minority and economically challenged communities—or only cover stories that pertain to crime. Seeing disproportionately low numbers of people of color in front of the camera, producing news, or in management positions can also reinforce negative perceptions (Rivas-Rodriguez, 2004).

In April 2011, the American Society of News Editors (ASNE) reported that the number of journalists of color working in newspaper and online newsrooms declined for the third consecutive year. Findings revealed that while minorities represent 36% of the U.S. population, they account for only 12.79% of journalists working in newspaper newsrooms (ASNE, 2011). The results are in sharp contrast with the organization's stated objectives. In 1978, ASNE set a goal to have minority journalists reach parity with their proportion of the U.S. population within 25 years (ASNE, 2012). In fact, based on disappointing results, the organization later voted to extend its deadline to the year 2025 (McGill, 2000). Additionally, the Radio Television Digital News Association (RTDNA) reported that the number of minorities employed in broadcast news has remained relatively flat for more than a decade (Papper, 2014).

Troy, a biracial student at Palo Alto High School, chooses not to actively participate in journalism. He noted, "You don't really see a ton of successful Black journalists that are in your face." These factors present additional challenges for teachers, because they can strengthen the fears of students who may already feel invisible and that their concerns do not matter.

The journalistic pedagogical approach seeks to benefit all students, regardless of their cultural backgrounds or professional ambitions. However, recruiting future journalists is not the objective. "I almost never talk about this as a career building program because what it offers is valuable in such a much wider variety of careers" says Paul Kandell at Palo Alto High School. "Some may go on to pursue professional journalism, but the vast majority don't—but they still value what they got here."

Students who do go on to choose journalism careers are often influenced by their scholastic journalism experiences. Kandell's colleague Ellen Austin, who is also an award-winning educator and serves on the regional board of the Journalism Education Association, says, "Fifty percent of future journalists start in high school and seventy-five percent of minority journalists start in high school."

Yet avoidance of journalism cuts deeper for some students. Troy explained that participation is considered out of step with the members of his primary peer group, who are mostly students of color: "Journalism isn't really an important thing and it seems like whitewashed or whatever it might be."

"Whitewashed" is a pejorative label some students of color ascribe to peers whom they believe "act White" or overly associate with White students. "I have been called 'whitewashed' before—but I don't feel too whitewashed," says Darci, an African American student at Paly who lives in East Palo Alto and serves on the staff of the school's broadcast news program. She added, "I've always hung out with different types of races, ethnicities—people. . . . Issues of race will always occur, it's just a thing that we have in our society. I think we just have to adapt and know who we are."

Marcus has experienced similar comments from some of his peers:

> I certainly deal with a lot of the "whitewash" thing at Paly, because most of my friends, well, not most my friends, but I have a lot of friends who are White, and have a lot of friends who are Black also. And so you kind of have to build a balance because there's a pretty big division between Black and White. . . . There are people who eat lunch on one side of the quad and people who eat lunch on the other side. People who eat lunch on one side are on publications and the people who eat lunch on the other side aren't.

It may be surprising to some that race remains such a polarizing factor in relations between millennial teenagers in a cosmopolitan community so associated with innovation and progressive politics. Yet these tensions can be traced to historical and structural factors that can adversely affect the area's current generation of students. Redlining, the systematic practice of denying people of color the right to purchase homes in White communities, was prevalent in the region until it was outlawed in 1977. The practice suppressed racial integration and economic diversity (Cutler, 2015).

School busing was implemented in many communities across the nation to counter inequities, yet its benefits and disadvantages are still heavily debated. Although the practice can provide disenfranchised students with access to schools with more resources, some critics argue the advantages come with costs (Morris, 2009; Seelye, 2012). Despite best intentions, students who travel from economically challenged to more affluent communities can carry an unwarranted sense of shame (Goins, 2008) and isolation (Ayscue & Orfield, 2014).

Additionally, peer pressures can create tension. Few teenagers want to engage in practices that are considered "uncool." Controversial and often cited research suggests that some high-achieving minority students bear the burden of being ridiculed by peers who equate studious behavior with "acting White" (Fordham & Ogbu, 1986). More recent research questions this premise, suggesting that these frictions have more to do with class struggle than with race. Cliques of all varieties are common in high schools. Spending ability affects the range of activities available to students, and it can shape their social interactions and curricular choices (McMahon, 2012; Tyson et al., 2005).

Before joining the University of Oregon, Dr. Karla Kennedy taught journalism-oriented ELA courses at Miami Norland Senior High School. The student body there is predominately African American, and she describes her former students as very engaged. "I haven't found students of color to be less interested in learning or in journalism. It has more to do with whether they feel a part of the school community," Kennedy said.

By necessity, journalistic learning extends into after school assignments where students research topics, conduct interviews, and assemble publications. Students who attend school close to home are not burdened by the transportation issues and safety concerns that can make participation difficult for those who commute from farther away.

Paul Kandell explained how these issues affect minority participation within Palo Alto High's journalism courses. "They may be the only student from EPA on the staff. They might be younger than everyone else on the staff. So, no pre-established friends, no one who looks like them on the staff—so no natural companions, if you will," Kandell said.

His colleague, Ellen Austin, agreed. "Minority students have said, 'Ms. Austin, I would be in that class but it's snowing in there—it's so White.'" You're not going to be able to change the core culture—you have to do it in alternate ways.

Regardless of students' reasoning, these issues are problematic for educators who are sincerely committed to building a fully inclusive campus community.

With the exception of overt bigotry, social psychologists generally favor the practice of allowing space for students' varying perspectives to be expressed—even if they are unpopular, or are at odds with their teacher's personal views (Villegas & Lucas, 2002; Wentzel, 1997). Immediate invalidation of a student's belief system rarely changes his or her opinion. We lead by example, and by providing opportunities for students to broaden their thinking.

Publication, the mass sharing of student work, is one of the key factors that distinguishes journalistic assignments from conventional homework—and its effect can be powerful for students, as Troy later discovers. A race-related incident at a campus basketball game led him to make a public statement in the student-published *Viking* sports magazine. The publication's cover story reported that after one of the school's Caucasian players dunked the ball, a large section of seniors chanted, "He's-a-White-guy! He's-a-White-guy!" The chant was directed at the junior class and two African American players who had failed their dunks. The magazine's cover featured Troy's portrait among a multitude of other diverse students. Within the pages he stated, "When [people] see Black players, they think 'an unintelligent player' and 'ridiculously athletic.' Grades are more important to me."

In this instance, the published story functioned as a tool for the effective mediation of a matter that could have escalated and caused lasting ill will across campus. The story buffered tensions by allowing students to articulate varying perspectives in a respectful and orderly fashion. Troy reflected on the experience and sought to clearly articulate his point of view. This is consistent with the writing standards for 11th and 12th graders that relate to presenting ideas.

EAST PALO ALTO SUMMER PROGRAM: IMPACTING DIVERSITY

Sometimes cultural divides call for more decisive action. Concerns about the lack of diversity in the journalism-oriented ELA courses at Palo Alto High led Paul Kandell to raise grant funds to establish a 6-week summer

---

COMMON CORE STRATEGIES

The Common Core places calls for students to proficiently do the following:

- Present an opinion that is tied to and reflects on experiences, observations, or resolutions.
- Produce clear and well-reasoned writing that is developed, organized, and presented in a style that is appropriate to task, purpose, and audience.

To support the development of these skills, consider how breaking news stories can potentially be "teachable moments." Stories unfolding in distant places may mirror local concerns and become a catalyst for discussion, reading, writing, and local comparisons. Civil unrest following the summer 2014 shooting of an unarmed African American teenager by a white police officer in Ferguson, Missouri, brought race relations into national consciousness. It also sparked a public debate about whether suburban and rural law enforcement is becoming over-militarized. Such incidents can be starting points for students to explore how these matters play out within their own communities.

---

media arts program in East Palo Alto's neighborhood Boys and Girls Club. Kandell and Austin see it as a safe and familiar place for students of color to experience the potential benefits of journalistic learning, away from the scrutiny of the peers who might ridicule them. Cohorts average 12–14 students, enlisted from several high schools in the area that have students who are bused from East Palo Alto. Internship time is split between *East Palo Alto Today*, a bimonthly community newspaper and online website, and the Midpeninsula Media Center, which is the Palo Alto area's public access cable television facility. Participating students, for whom income from summer jobs can be critical, receive a small stipend.

The East Palo Alto summer program requires a significant commitment. Kandell handles all fundraising and recruitment and manages its bare-bones budget. The instructor team allocates minimal compensation for themselves and forfeit a good portion of the summer break.

Despite the name "East" Palo Alto, the city is due north of its affluent neighbor and is its own incorporated community. East Palo Alto has often made news due to high crime and poverty. Crime is a relevant part of East Palo Alto's story, but it is not the only story. Key to the success of the program is allowing students to find value in their community, in the midst of such negativity. This is accomplished through partnerships with community news organizations like *East Palo Alto Today*. Publisher Henrietta Burroughs is a seasoned professional who left mainstream media to focus on filling a void she found within the community. In the decade it has existed, the publication's focus has been reporting a more diverse range of news, including inspiring stories that would otherwise not be covered.

Burroughs says the internships provide tangible and lasting benefits: "I think the value shows up in being able to communicate well, in terms of knowing how to talk to anybody. So, these are valuable skills whether you want to be a journalist or not."

Grassroots community-based internship programs can introduce students to journalistic learning opportunities that are less intimidating than what they might encounter in mainstream media organizations. Shiny corporate headquarters can seem foreign and sharply different from the students' own experiences. Grassroots efforts can become a gateway to mainstream media opportunities.

East Palo Alto Today is not equipped with state-of-the-art computers and software, but it is a place where students can engage in journalistic learning and take pride in the positive aspects of their community.

Darci participated in the East Palo Alto summer program and was among several students I interviewed who affirmed its benefits. "I used to think journalism was just writing. I liked writing but I wasn't the best writer. But taking beginning journalism over the summer helped me improve my writing a lot," she stated, and added, "Before I would get 'Cs' and now, through the year, I get 'As' on my writing."

Celina is Latina, an East Palo Alto resident, and in the summer program. She is a second-year student at Palo Alto High and sees long-term benefits from journalistic learning: "I find it really appealing, just because it's kinda front row to history in the process—and I find that very intriguing."

The East Palo Alto summer program offers an effective strategy for students who might otherwise not find the courage to explore journalistic learning. The program allows students to "test the waters" through exposure to new genres, and many have subsequently continued to participate during the academic year.

Kandell is pleased with results. "They are small numbers but considering the numbers in the program, and to have five or six from Paly . . . watching them succeed is pretty cool."

Austin shared why she has sacrificed several summers to co-facilitate: "I do this program because I believe in what we are trying to do here. . . . I believe that these are the building blocks, not for 'jobs,' but for forming a better-woven social fabric."

Such endeavors serve to stimulate civic engagement and empower teachers to draw on untapped resources within their communities. They allow students to explore contemporary themes that are unfolding within their counties, cities, and neighborhoods. This instruction can bridge gaps between classrooms and communities, providing a wealth of interaction and learning. The approach is effective in socioeconomically depressed communities, where teachers face formidable challenges. Despite adversity, educators need not fall victim to their circumstances. They can gain support by collaborating with colleagues and parents who may have relationships they can leverage. Funding and resource support can be found through ingenuity and perseverance.

REFLECTIONS ON SHARING

The East Palo Alto summer program's success underscores the merits of integrating journalistic learning strategies into regular ELA classes, rather than marginalizing them as electives, after-school programs, or other extracurricular programs. Alternative programs can be highly effective. However, lack of funds, transportation issues, and time demands can

---

TECHNOLOGY TIP

Summer programs and media internships may not be practical options in some communities due to location or safety concerns. Consider inviting media professionals to interact with students via Skype or Google Hangout. Identify prospective guests through alumni or parents. LinkedIn has a feature that allows searches filtered according to alumni affiliation, profession, and employer. Look for media experts from diverse backgrounds to foster equity and inclusion.

---

strain well-intentioned initiatives and result in diminishing returns. The real objective is to create a climate of full inclusion during the school day.

When teachers and administrators commit to fully incorporating journalistic strategies into the school day, it sends a strong message to students and parents that a spirit of collaboration and sharing will drive instruction. The result is higher levels of engagement. Students of color, like all students, stand to blossom from experiencing that their words can make a difference—among their peers and within their communities.

Other segments of a school's students may experience stress related to cultural stereotypes and societal expectations. Characterizations that suggest "otherness" fail to honor the whole child.

TAKEAWAYS

Focus on inclusivity.

- Acknowledge the demographic shifts occurring and consider how to best create a learning setting that is welcoming for all.
- Create assignments that encourage students from diverse backgrounds to become better acquainted and to honor their differences.

Consider creating a side program.

- Motivate hesitant writers by inviting them to suggest subjects they are truly passionate about.
- Partner with colleagues to introduce an after-school or summer program.

See controversies as "teachable moments."

- Recognize challenging topics and situations as potential openings for growth and understanding among students and faculty.
- Yet respect students' boundaries; do not force-feed issues.

RESOURCES

Watch Paul Kandell and Ellen Austin work with students in the East Palo Alto summer program: journalisticlearning.org/journalisticlearning.org/Diversity.html

Apple Education Leaders on iTunes: itunes.apple.com/us/itunes-u/learning-snapshots/id395854865?mt=10

Adobe Education Exchange: edex.adobe.com

CHAPTER FIVE

Collaboration

Sharing Curricular Power
and Digital Technology

Every person has a story, but most times those stories aren't getting acknowledged. . . . When I was really little, people always told me I couldn't do things. It was always: "you can't draw, you can't write, you can't do math." People tried to push me against the wall and tell me what I couldn't do.

—Olivia, senior at Roosevelt High School, Portland, OR

Olivia's story is not unlike those of many young people who have felt undervalued and unheard. Living without privilege and troubled by complicated home lives, these students carry extra burdens to school each day. Yet, public education is duty-bound to serve and enrich their lives.

Two years of studying Palo Alto High School's stellar campus-based and outreach programs inspired me to explore how less privileged communities might stand to benefit from some of the school's practices. Further research led me to the Journalism Education Association, where I discovered and interviewed numerous other teachers cited within these pages who lead highly successful programs at other schools.

As I have noted, scholastic journalism has a rich tradition on the campuses of many high schools across the nation. However, at most, it is an afterthought—divorced from the mainstream curriculum. Journalism often exists as an underfunded newspaper that is cobbled together after school, as an elective that "doesn't count" toward English credits, or as an extension of the yearbook club. Witnessing how students blossom when encouraged to write and report about their interests, concerns, and experiences inspired me to investigate possibilities for the broader adoption of journalistic learning strategies.

The Common Core State Standards—with its shift in emphasis toward deeper exploration of nonfiction text, media, and technology—opens a door. The relevance of journalism is implied in its preamble:

> To be ready for college, workforce training, and life in a technological so-
> ciety, students need the ability to gather, comprehend, evaluate, synthesize,
> and report on information and ideas, to conduct original research in order to
> answer questions or solve problems, and to analyze and create a high volume
> and extensive range of print and nonprint texts in media forms old and new.
> The need to conduct research and to produce and consume media is embed-
> ded into every aspect of today's curriculum. In like fashion, research and
> media skills and understandings are embedded throughout the Standards
> rather than treated in a separate section. (CCSS-ELA, p. 4)

Although the Common Core advocates for broader media and technology integration, as a practical matter many school districts lack the financial
resources to fulfill that promise. Overburdened teachers and administrators can view this aspect of the guidelines as "another thing" to add to an
already lengthy to-do list, rather than be inspired to find creative ways to
meet the challenge.

This chapter suggests affordable strategies for integrating more technology in ELA courses, with a specific emphasis on digital storytelling.
It chronicles my research team's work at Roosevelt High School in Portland, Oregon, where we applied many of the techniques I discovered at
Palo Alto High School and from other educators interviewed for this
book. Additionally, the chapter explores new approaches to professional
development and provides resources where teachers can find support. It
discusses how to create alliances with colleges and universities, and how
to access donated and free technology.

MEDIA LITERACY AND DIGITAL SKILLS

Millennial students are often referred to as *digital natives*, students who
have been raised with technology. Unlike their predecessors, they live in
an information-saturated world and have different sensibilities, expectations, and learning styles (Palfrey & Gasser, 2008; Prensky, 2001). The
Pew Internet and American Life project confirms that more than one-
half of all teens have created media content and that one-third who use
the Internet share what they produce. They create and exchange photo-
graphs, videos, and text (Pew Internet Research, 2005, 2010).

You need look no further than the ever-increasing pervasiveness of
visual media—and particularly video—to understand its vital relevance
as tool for present-day effective communication: YouTube, Skype, Face-
Time, Twitter's Vine, Instagram's Hyperlapse—video is everywhere.

However, when the topic of technology is raised the conversation usually turns to access. There is a tendency to frame discussions around the "haves" and the "have-nots," often referred to as the "digital divide" (Compaine, 2001; Norris, 2001). For several decades federal studies showed vast disparities between affluent urban dwellers and those living in poor rural communities, in terms of online connectivity and personal computer ownership. Studies revealed that Whites, males, the wealthy, the college educated, and people under the age of 55 were the primary users of new technologies (U.S. Department of Commerce, 1995, 1998, 1999, 2000).

In 2004, the annual Freshman Survey indicated the gap in computer use was widening significantly between African American students and their peers (Farrell, 2005). Several newer studies reveal continuing disparities, factored by race, gender, socioeconomic status, geographic locale, English fluency, disability, education level, and age (Fox, 2007; Pew Internet and American Life Project, 2007).

However, a second wave of scholarship reframes the issue of the "digital divide," focusing more on gaps related to skills and use rather than access. Measures are generally limited to how many schools have what number of computers and broadband access, without a deeper investigation of the pedagogical practices within schools that stratify some students in compromising ways. Goode (2010) argues that proficient use of technology is an "invisible academic prerequisite" for students entering college (p. 584). Completing forms, enrolling in courses, accessing announcements, and participating in course-related discussions all require online navigation skills.

Jenkins (2009) asserts that it is a misnomer to think that youths acquire new technology skills and competencies on their own. He has advanced the notion that students need to acquire *digital literacies*, in order to thrive in this new environment. Jenkins argues, "Access to this participatory culture functions as a new form of the hidden curriculum, shaping which youth will succeed and which will be left behind as they enter school and the workplace" (p. xii).

Many of the new digital literacy skills Jenkins describes correlate to what students encounter with journalistic learning strategies and are aligned with the Common Core, including the following:

- ***Collective Intelligence***—the ability to pool knowledge and compare notes with others toward a common goal.
- ***Judgment***—the ability to evaluate the reliability and credibility of different information sources.

- ***Transmedia Navigation***—the ability to follow the flow of stories and information across multiple modalities.
- ***Networking***—the ability to search for, synthesize, and disseminate information.
- ***Negotiation***—the ability to travel across diverse communities, discerning and respecting multiple perspectives, and grasping and following alternative norms. (p. xiv)

Mobile devices are leveling the playing field and democratizing Internet access. It is estimated that the number of people coming online will have jumped from 1.8 billion in 2010 to 5 billion globally by 2020 (Diamandis, 2014). Among U.S. teens, 78% own cellphones, and nearly half (47%) of them own smartphones. That equates to 37% of all teens owning smartphones, up from just 23% in 2011. One in four teens (23%) owns a tablet computer (Pew Internet Research, 2013). The exponential growth of mobile devices becomes clearer when you consider that Apple sold 25 times more CPU transistors during the weekend it launched the iPhone 6 than were in all PCs on Earth in 1995 (Diamandis, 2014). However, without teachers guiding students in how to maximize the educational benefit of these devices, we risk that their greater potential will go untapped.

Aligned with the journalistic learning strategies outlined in this book is a growing *media literacy* movement intent on teaching students to become more proficient at accessing, analyzing, evaluating, and communicating information. A key emphasis is on empowering students to be critical thinkers and creative producers (NAMLE, 2015). Hobbs (2007), one of the founders of the movement, has documented how media literacy significantly improves reading comprehension, critical analysis, and related academic skills. It also catalyzes motivation and teaches capable citizenship.

Yet some educators may fail to see the value of teaching media skills, such as digital storytelling through use of video—presuming it has little to do with "real writing." However, a growing body of research supports its efficacy. Digital storytelling has shown the potential to enhance student engagement (Brass, 2008; Lambert, 2007), promote agency and authorship of identities (Hull & Katz, 2006), and provide students with opportunities to express themselves in multimodal and authentic ways (Short & Kauffman, 2000). In ELA classrooms, it encourages personal writing, reflexivity about relationships, and civic engagement (Jacobs, 2011). Dr. Karla Kennedy, my colleague on the Roosevelt High School project, notes, "It's just another extension for them. It teaches them to go out now and say 'I can not only write about it, but how can I put visualization to it? How can I make my story come to life even more?' So it takes them to another level of saying 'how can I tell this story better?'"

Video is not new. We have had television since the 1940s. But *we* did not have it; barons of industry controlled the ability to transit moving images. What is new is the vast numbers of people who now have high-definition (HD) video cameras in their pockets and the power to instantaneously share what they shoot globally. Miniaturization, image stabilization technology, and lower costs empower amateurs to mimic pros.

Think about how the invention of the printing press democratized access to knowledge, and how desktop publishing democratized the ability to create knowledge, and you get a sense of the power and significance of the present video revolution.

Business presentations with static Microsoft PowerPoint slides are passé. Organizations and other entities, private and public, are turning to video to more effectively tell their stories. Video has the power to strike an emotional chord and move people to take action. Donors write checks, prospects make purchases, and social activism makes a difference.

A common fear is that visual storytelling will displace writing, but it will not. Written words remain vital. They provide context and subtext, and they inspire our imagination in distinctly different ways. Further, strong writing shapes many of the best video presentations. Typically, visual stories follow a path—from concept to text to several rewrites—before making it to a screen. Effective video editors know how to craft a compelling narrative arc—to create tension and build suspense—much like talented writers. However, just as owning a computer and word processing software does not make you a good writer, having an HD video camera in your pocket does not make you an effective visual storyteller. Writing and videography are similar, but distinct crafts that require training and practice. Yet a lack of resources and support limit teachers' ability to learn and teach digital journalism skills in our schools.

As a researcher, I saw an opportunity to mitigate these obstacles by working to identify possible interventions where cost and time investments from school districts would be minimal. I assembled an eight-person research and outreach team, composed of interested graduate and undergraduate students within our University of Oregon journalism school, and consulted colleagues in our College of Education. Tapping local university talent is an effective strategy that can easily be replicated.

We collaborated for a year to identify core components of what worked in successful programs, and to develop a new curriculum that could be piloted in schools where journalism was limited or nonexistent.

We were particularly interested in addressing the needs of underserved students living in urban and rural areas, and in identifying a school within Oregon where we could run a pilot project. We found grant funding within our university to support our work.

I share insights from our research phase here to shed light on curriculum development processes that are rarely revealed to frontline educators. It is not uncommon for researchers to design educational materials in ways that are not transparent to the teachers who will actually use them. This can lead to the handing down of curricula that are well intended but that may seem out of sync with the realities of the classroom experience. A greater objective is to inspire educators to experiment with these ideas to develop their own curricula. Students benefit when teachers tailor coursework to meet local needs and draw from community resources.

Having an institutional commitment to innovation can open new possibilities in the advancement of education. We created alliances between the University of Oregon School of Journalism and Communication and the College of Education to foster new opportunities for interdisciplinary experimentation. In this instance, our overarching commitment was to positively impact student outcomes by better preparing educators to teach new digital skills, all in accordance with the Common Core State Standards.

In addition to what we learned from Palo Alto High and other outstanding programs, we drew from our own experiences. Our journalism school is acknowledged nationally for its innovative approaches to integrating digital skills training into the college-level curriculum. In spring 2011, my students were the first at any university to create an iPad magazine using new digital tools from Adobe. *OR Magazine* continues to win awards and accolades for its numerous innovations in digital publishing (CSPA, 2014, 2015; Reimold, 2013). However, gadgetry is always a secondary element in our pedagogical approach. Our emphasis is primarily on developing critical thinkers, strong researchers, and solid writers who are prepared to use an ever-emerging array of technological tools. Ethical storytelling is the essence of what we teach.

We also place strong emphasis on "student voice." Students drive the leadership of many of our upper-level project-based courses. It is that "get them up in front of the room," and "empower leaders to be leaders" philosophy that Esther Wojcicki and Paul Kandell advocate that we also stress. When we follow this mantra, we find students take ownership of their learning in profound ways that lead to award-winning work.

Through our research, we noted several initiatives that seek to outfit the nation's public classrooms with new technology. In February 2014,

Apple pledged $100 million and Adobe $300 million respectively in technology support for the Obama administration's ConnectED program, with a goal to bring 99% of America's schools into the digital age (WhiteHouse.gov, 2014). The initiatives do offer some free support. Apple Distinguished Educators have created a series of downloadable resources available on iTunes, and Adobe Education Leaders offer numerous online tutorials through Adobe's Education Exchange. Both collections are thoughtfully prepared and clearly presented. However, most tend to *talk about* teaching, rather than show real teacher–student interactions in the classroom. We identified a significant missing link: teacher training. Without adequate professional development these and other substantial investments in technology integration risk falling short of their intended goals.

RETHINKING PROFESSIONAL DEVELOPMENT

My participation in both Apple and Adobe educator groups and my research studies informed our team's process as we began to explore fresh approaches to teacher training.

Our first step was to survey the landscape. We noted that professional development programs are often structured as one- or two-day in service sessions, where attendance is mandatory and the content is fairly predictable. The intent of these workshops is to spark innovation, bring about change in teachers' practices and attitudes, and impact student-learning outcomes. However, there is an entire body of research that shows most professional development programs fail to achieve these objectives (Cohen & Hill, 1998, 2000; Kennedy, 1998; Wang, Frechtling, & Sanders, 1999). Teachers leave with a few tips, some handouts, and perhaps a binder that ends up on a shelf.

Educational psychology professor Thomas R. Guskey, at the University of Kentucky, is among the most cited authorities on teacher training. He argues that "significant change in teachers' attitudes and beliefs occur primarily *after they gain evidence of improvements* in student learning" (Guskey, 2002, p. 383). Such evidence is difficult to present in conventional trainings where the participants are all other teachers. Topics like student engagement and strategies for stimulating critical thinking are talked about, but at a conceptual level. Short of role-plays, they are difficult to demonstrate.

Our team sought to set aside conventional notions about teacher training and to arrive at a new approach. To do so, we asked ourselves a series of questions: What if teachers had opportunities to not only witness the types of results considered vital by Guskey's research, but also to pause a training, review previous sections, and refer back to any part of it on demand?

It is a fair guess that our team's preliminary discussions were pointing us toward use of video. But we were mindful of its limitations. We acknowledged the value of human interaction in live trainings. Also, with Khan Academy and the previously mentioned online resources from Apple and Adobe, video materials seemed ubiquitous. However, despite this being the YouTube era, there was not much about the present methods, production, and presentation of instructional videos that we could point to as "innovative." We found conventional training videos to be unimaginative and uninspiring. Most were screencasts featuring an instructor talking over a collection of PowerPoint slides, or real-time recordings of training sessions that were poorly produced. If we were going to use video, we were intent on breaking the mold.

This led us to ask more questions. What if our "training" did not look or feel like a training? How might we avoid the monotonous styles of presentation so associated with the genre? Many were dull, with staged vignettes featuring bad actors. We wanted to capture authentic classroom interactions and to present them in thought-provoking and compelling ways.

Further, we questioned the standard practice of who leads trainings. Most workshop facilitators are skilled professionals. Yet we sought to supplement what they offer with alternative approaches that would potentially serve teachers in new and impactful ways.

Finally, we explored new strategies for providing teachers with ongoing support. A common complaint is that professional development is confined to occasional workshops, with little opportunity for follow-up. What if we could empower schools and their districts to create new structures for support that would not adversely impact their budgets?

These are tall orders that we attempted to tackle one by one. Our initial focus was on how we might provide teachers with evidence of student improvement. My previous professional background as a nonfiction television and documentary producer gave me firsthand knowledge about how to capture authentic moments on video. The ability to follow instructor–student interactions over a defined period of time would potentially allow viewers to witness academic growth.

Our intention was to capture the essential moments of our workshop on video to show teachers how to train their students to effectively use video to craft their own stories. Strategically, with a documentary approach, we would edit together and present only highlights from these interactions. This would save teachers from having to endure the monotony of real-time interludes that might be insignificant. Also, stylistically, we would not confine our cameras to a static position at the back of a classroom. We would move with the action, wherever it unfolded.

Along with our commitment to train teachers was an equal commitment to tell "good stories." Meaning, we would focus on "characters," embracing our culture's attraction to stories that have a strong narrative arc.

We recognized that compelling stories are the driving force behind reality and dramatic television. However, in authentic documentaries the stories are not concocted—they are real. An effective documentary has viewers empathize. It moves them to invest in the emotional growth of characters as each of their stories unfolds—over time. There was another distinction that became evident. Typically, a documentary's intent is to inform or to entertain, but rarely to do both simultaneously. In this regard, our interest was to blend the documentary and instructional genres to create something new: a character-driven instructional video. We began using the term *docu-instructional media*.

The "over time" aspect was another element we believed would distinguish our approach. We would certainly not be the first to document instructors interacting with students. However, most examples we found filmed isolated portions of a single lesson or class session, rather than a series of interactions that progressed over multiple and sequential days.

We theorized that another advancement in our docu-instructional media approach would be to rethink who should lead the instruction. University professors and professional development experts have much to offer teachers. However, we also had a team of very sharp and highly enthusiastic undergraduate journalism student volunteers, guided by a graduate student. All were eager to take the lead. We trusted they would bridge a generational gap and serve as role models for students who might not have parents or relatives who had attended college.

This approach was aligned with the theoretical frameworks that guided my initial research. *Self-determination Theory* (SDT) emphasizes the pedagogical value of three areas of support: *autonomy, competency,* and *relatedness* (Deci & Ryan, 2000, 2002). SDT involves empowering students of all ages to be independent thinkers, to develop confidence, and to establish trust. *Situated learning* (Lave & Wenger, 1991) and *communities of practice* (Wenger, 1998) are theoretical constructs that stress the significance of social-interactive learning. Simply put, our objective was to have slightly older mentors guide high school students through potentially transformational experiences.

If we were correct, our method could serve as a template for partnerships between journalism schools and high schools across the nation. We envisioned a league of volunteer college journalism students with a shared commitment to supporting underserved secondary-level teachers and students in their own communities. However, we were getting ahead of ourselves. First, we needed to pilot our ideas. We needed to identify a school in which to test our ideas.

DIGITAL LITERACY AND COLLABORATION CASE STUDY: ROOSEVELT HIGH

Our research team identified Roosevelt High in Portland, Oregon, as a school that could benefit from our pilot digital skills training project. We collaborated with Melody Hughes, a mid-career language arts teacher at the school, to plan a weeklong program that would give students opportunities to discover meaningful stories about members of their community and instill digital literacy skills.

We chose Roosevelt for several reasons. Situated in North Portland's St. Johns community, it is the most ethnically diverse high school in the state. Its student population is 31% Latino, 30% White, 23% African American, 9% Asian/Pacific Islander, and 4% Native American; 3% declare multiple races (Melton, 2010). With 84% of the school's students receiving free or reduced lunch, Roosevelt ranks among Oregon's poorest high schools (Parks, 2014). "There are definitely some challenges living in the community," says Hughes. "We're in a kind of low-income neighborhood that does have, in some pockets, a higher crime rate."

Additionally, Roosevelt students' standardized test scores have lagged behind state and local averages over the years, which Hughes partially attributes to socioeconomic pressures. "The expectation of testing and the reality of where our students are is sometimes mismatched, and that can be very frustrating for both staff and students," Hughes says. However, she has noticed a significant difference in the ways her students respond to journalistic teaching strategies. "With journalism, I see kids awaken in a way that I don't see in any other class because it's so real and tangible. They get to go talk to someone; they get to put together this story. And it's them driving the ship."

We also had preexisting relationships with administrators and faculty at the school. Dr. Karla Kennedy, our journalism school's outreach coordinator, spent a prior year working with Hughes and her students to revive its newspaper, which had not published since 1991. A team of

Roosevelt students earned their first bylines and experienced the rush of having peers read and talk about their work.

Kennedy is a former student publication adviser and has witnessed journalism's impact firsthand. "They get to understand why it's important to have voice, why it's important to be concerned with what's going on in your community, in your school, why is it important to hold on and have reins of your own education," Kennedy says.

However, when we proposed a digital storytelling pilot course for Hughes and her students for spring 2014, Roosevelt still lacked the resources to incorporate video production and digital storytelling into its curriculum. We saw an opportunity to explore the potential pedagogical benefits by creating an immersive experiential program, in accordance with the Common Core: The Standards stress that student be strategic and capable of using technology and digital media:

> Students employ technology thoughtfully to enhance their reading, writing, speaking, listening, and language use. They tailor their searches online to acquire useful information efficiently, and they integrate what they learn using technology with what they learn offline. They are familiar with the strengths and limitations of various technological tools and mediums and can select and use those best suited to their communication goals. (CCSS-ELA, p. 7)

In consultation with Hughes, we determined that a weeklong program would provide a sufficient amount time to introduce a series of digital storytelling skills and see tangible results without adversely impacting the school's tight academic calendar. However, a concern was that we would present a successful but isolated weeklong curriculum that might easily be forgotten. If possible, we wanted to make a lasting impact. This strengthened our commitment to documenting the highlights of our sessions on video. We wanted to preserve the most instructive and compelling moments as online modules, easily accessible by teachers and students at Roosevelt—and globally.

Additionally, we asked our journalism school to donate 20 used Apple iPod Touch devices that were scheduled for retirement. The choice made sense for several reasons. More than 100 million video-enabled iPod Touch devices have sold since they originally debuted in 2007, making older models easily obtainable at modest costs and even free. They are also easily outfitted with inexpensive accessory kits, and we found them to be fairly intuitive for most teachers and students to use.

The following subsections offer a descriptive account of our actual 5-day pilot project, with the intent of supporting educators to envision

---

TECHNOLOGY TIP

Many communities have recycling centers that collect, refurbish, and recirculate used electronic devices that would otherwise end up in landfills. Steve Glinberg, developer of KidCalc and several other popular education apps, runs a web-based recycling program specifically designed to provide teachers with previously owned iPads, iPhones, and iPod Touch devices. "I am amazed and inspired by the generosity I've seen since I began this iOS device recycling program," says Glinberg. "Recently I received a brand new unopened iPad in the mail. Hundreds of kids who otherwise wouldn't have the opportunity to interact with and be inspired by this new technology will, thanks to this and the many other generous donations" (Glinberg, 2013).

Additionally, reach out to journalism and media schools in your area about gear they may be retiring and mentorship support. Some higher education institutions offer their students community service credit.

---

how they might adapt it to fit their individual curricular needs. Each section can be expanded into multiple instructional sequences or modified to stand alone.

The workshop participants were 12 Roosevelt students and their teacher, Melody Hughes, mentored by four University of Oregon (UO) students and our instructional staff, which included Dr. Karla Kennedy, Maya Lazaro, and myself. Jordan Bentz, our videographer, was present to document the highlights. We intentionally structured the workshop to allow UO students to take the lead to bridge the generational gap between high school students and instructors.

Planning a Story

Roosevelt High is distinguished by its Colonial Revival–style façade, erected in 1921. Corinthian white columns frame the two-story red brick main building. It is the kind of classic structure you might expect to find in the heart of Virginia—not ultra-hip "Portlandia"—but this is a city of contradictions. Your eyes are drawn to the building's white colonial clock tower and steeple. The interior fixtures are also relics of a bygone era, yet there is a sense of everlasting architectural charm.

Twelve eager but cautious students file into to Melody Hughes's language arts classroom this spring Monday morning for Day One in our series of five sessions. They are a diverse mix of seniors and juniors—instinctively curious about what to expect. Leroy is a brawny and charismatic African American student in his senior year and is clearly popular among his peers. He is wearing a baseball cap turned backward and a varsity sweatshirt. During a brief aside, he tells our documentary crew interviewers why he is committed to learning new digital skills: "As of right now, my sisters are in foster care. I don't know if they actually remember me or if they know who I am. But I want to be a brother they would be proud of, so that's where the majority of my motivation comes from." It is a candid and unexpected moment that puts our project in proper perspective, reminding us why we are here.

Other students' distinct personalities begin to emerge. Maggie is a reserved but stylish senior who is Caucasian. Dark, long bangs, horn-rimmed glasses, and a small nose ring define her look—from the front. It's offset by the buzz cut that shapes the back of her hairstyle. "I like doing things more like independent . . . I guess," she says with nervous laughter.

Olivia comes across as more confident than the younger self she described as being rarely encouraged as a child. She is Caucasian and also stylish but chooses more traditional attire; she is more comfortable in a skirt and blouse with classic prints. She has long auburn hair. We learn that Olivia is a high achiever, in spite of the negative messages she received as a child.

Most members of the cohort have little or no previous experience with digital storytelling. Hughes and Kennedy have asked that they arrive prepared to talk about possible ideas for community-oriented stories that will translate well on video. The stories must be visually interesting.

Enthusiasm fills the air. "I was pretty excited," says Megan, another senior. Her dark blond hair is pulled back, revealing diamond-studded earrings and a hint of eyeliner.

"I came in here open-minded; ready to learn what you guys are ready to teach," says James, a lanky athlete with a light complexion, a slight case of acne, and a 1970s-style Afro. He is not easy to categorize, in terms of race or ethnicity.

As I recall these characteristics and commit them to paper, I sense my doubts about word choices and am confronted by the limitations of language. I struggle to search for words that will not trivialize the depth and significance of who these students are when you meet them in person. We are documenting these students' experiences, but this is not a reality show.

I know that written narratives help readers envision people and places they cannot see. Yet I do not wish to cast shadows or filter their authentic voices. First-person encounters seem closest to penetrating the interpersonal barriers we often impose on one another. This insight helps to explain the value of teaching digital storytelling.

Images have profound power.

Although photojournalists capture select moments of truth, video connects those moments to reveal a wide range of emotions and actions—as they occur—whether expressive or self-reflective. It speaks to what documentary video offers young storytellers: an opportunity to let audiences interpret and draw conclusions about the person featured with less filtering. Yes, lenses and lighting choices affect our perceptions. And yes, video editing—the process of reordering scenes and sequences—can color authenticity. However, there remains something pure and powerful about how video can capture reality. Done well, documentaries pierce through pretense and can challenge us to think.

Establishing project teams is the first order of business. Having an ability to collaborate is a fundamental learning objective of the Common Core. It states:

> Speaking and Listening standards require students to develop a range of broadly useful oral communication and interpersonal skills. Students must learn to work together, express and listen carefully to ideas, integrate information from oral, visual, quantitative, and media sources, evaluate what they hear, use media and visual displays strategically to help achieve communicative purposes, and adapt speech to context and task. (CCSS-ELA, p. 8)

Students are asked to break into story groups of three or four, and they are encouraged to self-select members they do not already know well. Separating cliques is a good practice because students with close ties often have trouble holding one another accountable. At least one member of each team should have a sense of self-confidence about working with technology. Organizing groups in this manner helps ease anxiety and fosters an environment where productivity can flourish.

Hughes, Kennedy, and several of our UO volunteers canvass the room and serve as mentors. However, they encourage the Roosevelt students to take the lead. Kennedy says, "This is the one class that asks you 'what do you think?' This is the one class where you pretty much run 75% of it. So, it's not come and look at something on the board—here's the problem—solve it. We're asking you to tell us what the problem is, so we can solve it together."

The teams begin to negotiate potential story selections. Several express a desire to shine a spotlight on unsung heroes. Megan and James are in a group that wants to profile Mel, an energetic senior citizen who contributes much of his time to volunteer work at Roosevelt. "He's been here since I was a freshman—and he comes over, cleans up, cuts the grass, and stuff that no one else wants to do," Megan says.

Realizing you can create awareness and make a difference through reporting and publishing is profoundly powerful for many students. In the process of finding their voice, many choose to share that power with others. "I want to do a profile on Nathan, one of my friends who is a musician," Leroy says. "Despite what he does for the school, nobody really knows about Nathan. He's not well known, and I feel like he should be."

Our mentors coach the students in selecting stories that will be visually interesting. They learn that when working with video, the potential impact of what is said heavily depends on what is seen.

Teams are encouraged to take the evening to carefully consider whether their proposed stories will be sufficiently visual and interesting.

Exploring a Story

The cohort returns the next morning ready to work. Today's first objective is to introduce basic interview skills. They will discover that being an effective interviewer is critical in journalism—especially when your medium is video. Forgetting to ask key questions can severely affect a story's impact. With a written story, you can call back later to clarify a point or ask for more details. However, with video going back is much more complicated.

COMMON CORE STRATEGIES

The process of pitching story ideas is aligned with the Standards that pertain to presentation skills. College- and career-ready students should proficiently:

- Present information, findings, and supporting evidence, convey a clear and distinct perspective, allowing listeners to follow the line of reasoning as well as alternative perspectives.

To build this proficiency, conduct practice brainstorm sessions where students introduce a topic of concern in their community. Have them list numerous ways to approach the story, remaining mindful of contrasting points of view. Identify appropriate individuals who can speak about the topic. What are potential ways to visualize the subject? Discuss possible uses of media that will best tell the story. Perhaps still images or music would enhance the projects.

Iris Bull, one of our UO graduate teaching fellows, walks to the front of the class. Students are seated in their groups. She asks students to pull out a pen and notepad. "For this next exercise, pick a member of your group as a partner. Preferably, someone you still don't know well," Bull says. "You'll split the next 10 minutes—5 minutes each—interviewing one another."

A key journalistic skill is learning to formulate questions that dig beneath the surface. Asking tough questions requires practice and contradicts much of how we are socialized to interact in society. Students are taught to be polite and to raise a hand before asking a question. Effective journalists probe and provoke—in a professional manner.

During an aside, Bull tells our documentary team, "I want them to talk. I want to put them outside their comfort zones." It's an essential leadership skill that can benefit students throughout their lives. We live in competitive times when shyness can be costly.

Olivia is teamed with Brandon and asks about his plans for the future. He shares about his personal ambitions and plans for college. Reflecting on the exercise, Olivia told our documentary crew, "When you do an interview you start with the general, 'who are you, what's your age, what's your name, where do you want to go to college?' But then you need to ask, 'Why do you want to go to that college? What was it that led you there?'"

Some students are surprised by what they discover. James learns that outward appearances do not always reveal underlying truths. "I was interviewing the leader of our group, Megan," says James. "I always thought

---

COMMON CORE STRATEGIES

This exercise aligns with the Common Core that address speaking and listening standards:

- Initiate and participate effectively in a range of collaborative discussions (one on one, in groups, teacher led) with diverse partners on grades 11–12 topics, texts, and issues, building on others' idea and expressing their own clearly and persuasively.

To nurture growth, have students take turns leading discussion groups. During each student's turn as leader, he or she is to stand before the group, maintain order and fairness, and keep time. Leaders are to end the round by summarizing the various perspectives expressed. Group participants are to end each round by offering the leader constructive criticism.

she was from an upbringing family with college degrees, but she [will be] a first-generation college student—on the way." It is easy to assume differences rather than explore common connections. Economic challenge is a thread that connects many of these students.

Following a break, the afternoon turns to introducing students to the grammar of visualization. The cohort discovers similarities drawn from their knowledge of writing. A written story often begins with expository information, describing its setting. Similarly, videos often start with *wide shots* (also called establishing shots), which give viewers a sense of place.

Next, written stories seek to familiarize us with characters. We are introduced to a protagonist, antagonist, and other key players. In similar fashion, videos employ *medium shots* (head and shoulder length) to give us an initial sense of whom the story is about.

Revealing the plot or dilemma facing characters in written narratives is synonymous with use of *close-up* shots in video—bringing us closer into the story. Tension and plot twists described on a page translate into use of *extreme close-up* shots in video.

Bull demonstrates these distinctions by rapidly walking up to the students, with her boxed-formed hands closing tighter. "Wide shot, medium shot, close-up, extreme close-up," Bull says, now within inches of Maggie's startled face.

Bull stresses again that their video stories must be visual. "We need to see people engaged in 'doing,' rather than just talking," she reiterates.

"I want to do a story on a vet clinic," Maggie says. She's aware of a Roosevelt alumnus who now works as a technician at a veterinarian clinic not far from the school. Bull commends her for choosing a story that will include animals. Scenes with dogs and other pets usually provide good *b-roll* (action footage used to cover talking) opportunities.

Next, students are introduced to the gear. Groups are given bags containing an iPod Touch, a tripod, and an accessory kit that includes lens attachments and a plug-in microphone. They are invited to take the gear home and to begin experimenting. Day Three's session will delve deeper into how to make best use of the technology.

A more pressing order of business is teaching students to visualize— how to imagine their video stories in advance. Bull hands out blank storyboard forms (easily found through a Google search), which have rows of boxes for students to draw stick figures as they imagine various elements of their stories.

Leroy's story about his musician friend will require *close-up shots* of hands strumming the guitar and *establishing shots* that give us a sense of place. Leroy sketches how he envisions key sequences. The paper drawings allow students to stretch their imaginations before grounding their ideas in reality. They learn to explore what is possible before arriving at what is probable. It also saves time. Rather than overshoot or miss critical aspects of the story, they will go into to their productions with a stronger sense of what they need to capture.

Having coached students to commit their ideas to paper, next Bull challenges the cohort to consider the logistics associated with actually making a video. Unless it involves a breaking news story, it is generally inappropriate to show up unannounced where someone works or lives with a video camera. Bull stresses the need to connect with subjects in advance to lock down times, locations, and permission to shoot.

This discussion can provoke anxiety. High school students are not accustomed to making cold calls to people they have never met. It can seem counterintuitive because of the "don't talk to strangers" mantra echoed by so many parents. Yet, it is a vital skill that can build confidence and ease students out of their protective shells.

Teaching hundreds of undergraduates at the university level, I observe many students who share an aversion to making phone calls—preferring text messaging and emails instead. "They never answered my email" is a common explanation I hear for why certain students have trouble confirming their stories. I will ask them how likely they are to respond to emails from someone they have never met. With some reluctance, they get the message. Setting up an interview requires a detailed conversation.

Maggie nervously places a call to the clinic. "Hi, I'm a student journalist at Roosevelt High and I want to do a video story there," Maggie says. The friendly response she receives sets her at ease. The school bell rings, and our second day has ended.

The ability to "talk to strangers" is aligned with the Common Core's Speaking and Listening Standards:

> Students adapt their communication in relation to audience, task, purpose, and discipline. They set and adjust purpose for reading, writing, speaking, listening, and language use as warranted by the task. They appreciate nuances, such as how the composition of an audience should affect tone when speaking and how the connotations of words affect meaning. (CCSS-ELA, p. 8)

Documenting the Story

Teams return Wednesday morning, eager to begin shooting their stories. Some experimented with the camera gear overnight—but there is much to still learn. Alex, Jonas, and Alan—three talented undergraduate student volunteers from our journalism school—are on hand to mentor the teams. They will guide the Roosevelt students through deeper demonstrations about the video equipment.

Each group is asked to open their gear bags and remove the items. Out come an iPod Touch, lens attachments, a microphone, and a tripod. The lens attachments screw on to allow for wide angle or telephoto (close-up) shooting, as needed. The microphones are smaller than an index finger, and have a swivel base that simply snaps into the headphone jack on the side of an iPod Touch. (See the Need Tech video at digitalskillsworkshop.com for specific information about gear and accessories.)

Although students may be accustomed to shooting handheld videos with cameras and phones, they learn that tripods are essential for effective digital storytelling. The objective is to stabilize the picture so that viewers are not distracted by shaky shots. "You want them invested in characters, not preoccupied by the mechanics," Bull says. Think of it like intentionally removing unnecessary words and phrases that might obscure the impact of an otherwise cogent story. Costing just under $20, inexpensive tripods are well worth the investment.

Students frequently lose sight of the importance of capturing good audio. Your visuals can be spectacular, but your story will severely suffer if the audio is poor. The swivel snap-in microphones are directional, providing a higher quality of audio than the built-in microphone on iPod Touch devices.

Next, mentors demonstrate proper setup and framing of shots for on-camera interviews. "You want the camera at eye level," says Alex, one of our mentors, as he coaches Olivia to raise the height of her group's tripod.

Discussions turn to proper framing. Students new to video often make the mistake of positioning subjects in the center of the screen. However, in photography and video subjects appear aesthetically more pleasing when they are positioned off-center. Bull explains that this aesthetic principle is called the *rule-of-thirds.* To understand the concept, you need only take a standard 8.5″ by 11″ blank sheet of paper in landscape position and draw two equally distant vertical lines. Next, draw two equally distant horizontal lines, as you would if you were using an entire page to play tic-tac-toe.

The rule of thirds states that large masses (faces, people, and objects) look best when they fall along where any of the lines intersect (see Figure 5.1). When shooting video interviews, it is appropriate to position your subject to the left or right of center, depending on direction of his or her eyes.

Figure 5.1. Rule of Thirds Grid and Example

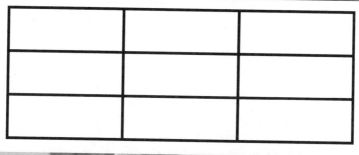

"We call this 'nose-room,'" says Bull. "You want to leave more space in front of the direction your subject is looking, and a slight bit of head room."

Armed with the basics of visual grammar, the teams are now ready to venture out and begin production, with our documentary crew following close behind.

Maggie arrives at the vet clinic ready to film but encounters potential obstacles she had not expected. Understandably, the clinic's management wants to protect the privacy of their clients. There is also concern that allowing cameras in the operating rooms might cause animals unnecessary anxiety. So, they insist on restricting what and where she can shoot. Maggie will have to conduct the interview in an empty examination room and limit "b-roll" filming to the lobby area.

Maggie could easily have felt discouraged—and might have considered abandoning the story altogether. However, such scenarios offer great opportunities for students to learn problem-solving skills.

COMMON CORE STRATEGIES

This process aligns with the Common Core Writing Standards that call for students to do the following:

- Use narrative techniques such as dialogue, pacing, description, reflection, and multiple plot lines to develop experiences, events, and/or characters.
- Use a variety of techniques to organize events so they build on one another to create an understandable whole and build toward a particular tone (for example, a sense of mystery, suspense, growth, or resolution).

Prepare students for making distinctions about effective strategies for telling stories visually by screening examples of short films and documentaries. Have them use pen and paper to note how filmmakers use varying camera angles to foreshadow, reveal, and add tension. Observe how secondary and parallel storylines are effectively used. Have students study how camera use can evoke emotions. Note that individuals can appear menacing when a camera looks at them from below. Conversely, individuals can appear less significant when a camera looks down on them.

A quick brainstorming session with her group and mentors leads Maggie to consider several workable solutions. The vet technician she is profiling agrees to bring her own dog to a park near Roosevelt after work. Maggie discovers that the tech rescued the dog—adding an unexpected dimension to the story. The outcome is much better than she originally imagined. Maggie captured great footage of the two playing outdoors in natural light and added a humanitarian angle to the piece.

Megan's team interviews Mel in a quiet classroom on campus and captures great footage of him walking through the main hallway at Roosevelt as he interacts with students and administrators. He also provides the team with personal photos of himself in his youth. Leroy is equally satisfied by the variety of shots sequences he captures of Nathan playing guitar. It is the end of a long day. Most of the assignments required time commitments that extended well after school.

Similar to writing, digital storytelling involves making choices about narrative structure, emphasis, pace, and tone.

Editing the Story

Thursday's focus is on video editing—putting the pieces of the story together. Much like a writer works to refine scattered ideas into well-crafted paragraphs and sentences, digital storytellers work to mold fragmented sound bites and images into a compelling video story. Maya Lazaro, our project coordinator, explains, "They are going through the footage and seeing what works and what doesn't work—this quote is more interesting than that quote. This shot more interesting than another." Students will use Roosevelt's Apple MacBooks, which come with iMovie-editing software (which is highly intuitive).

Alan Sylvestre, another of our undergraduate mentors, leads students in a basic overview of editing principles. "A-roll is typically the interview. When we're building our project, it is the main (and first) track that we reference, and everything is built upon it. And the b-roll is the action footage we place on top of the a-roll to help build the story."

Alan further explains there are several phases to the editing process. "We listen to the interview because it drives the narrative arc of our story. Then we review the action footage that we have to lay over the top. . . . Does it make sense with what they are saying?" He adds that it is often best to begin a story with a *wide* (establishing) *shot*, to give the audience a sense of place, before transitioning into closer shots.

Olivia compares the process to editing written work. "When it comes to stories, I've always been huge on editing. So once I got to that part of the process I was really comfortable." Maggie adds, "It's taken a while, but it's been fun knowing that I made this video."

Students will have one more opportunity to polish their work on the final day of the workshop. Some will have to scramble to gather additional footage to fill gaps in their stories. The entire cohort's efforts will culminate on Friday during an informal screening for invited guests. As discussed, editing video is much like editing words.

Refining and Sharing the Story

It's the final day, and there is much still to accomplish. As discussed in Chapter 1, the publishing of student work is one of the key factors that distinguishes journalistic learning from other pedagogical approaches. Public sharing raises the stakes and has students invest more in their work.

Students know that the results of the workshop will be posted to the Web, but our team intends to have them experience a more immediate

---

COMMON CORE STRATEGIES

Support students in learning visual grammar that reinforces the Common Core's writing standards. College- and career-ready students are expected to proficiently do the following:

- Introduce a topic; organize complex ideas, concepts, and information so that each new element builds on what precedes it to form a unified whole; include formatting, graphics, and multimedia when useful.

Screen additional short films and documentaries in class and ask students to keep a close eye on the editing. Have students note how shot lengths and use of music can affect a story's pace and tone. Draw comparisons between short shots and short sentences. Their staccato nature enhances the pace of a story, in contrast with longer shots and lengthier sentences. Make note of how filmmakers arrange shots in a sequence. Typically the earliest shots are like expository writing, providing audiences with a sense of place and time.

---

sense of satisfaction and acknowledgment. The final day is organized as a festive celebration. Earlier in the week they were given invitations to share with family, friends, and the individuals they profiled.

Anticipation runs high, as only an hour remains before guests are to arrive. Our journalism school covered catering costs. A team is setting out food and beverages, as students make final tweaks to their stories. Several eyes monitor the ticking wall clock.

"It's been a whirlwind to see their projects develop," Bull says. "I didn't think I was going to cry today, and I got to do that because one of the stories really was that powerful."

Mel is among the guests who file into the crowded classroom and take their seats before the lights are dimmed. Each student comes to the front to introduce his or her story. And each story receives a resounding round of applause. "Thank you—thank you all," Mel says as everyone turns to acknowledge him.

Next, the students take a bow, as the room applauds their accomplishments. "I'll take away that I really feel confident that I was able to do it," Olivia says. "From the very beginning, we chose the stories—and then following all the way to the end."

"It's awesome," Karla Kennedy says, "it's that light bulb that goes on in their heads, it's all of a sudden this whole brightness."

The final day of presentations is aligned with the Common Core's emphasis on presentation of knowledge and ideas.

Two months later, our camera crew returns to Roosevelt as many of our workshop participants are preparing to graduate. Students assemble in the cafeteria and assist one another in adjusting caps and straightening gowns. A sense of accomplishment fills the air.

We learn about many of their plans for the future. These students have been diligent at applying themselves during their four years at Roosevelt, and for many the hard work has resulted in special awards and scholarships. Leroy has received a Bill and Melinda Gates Foundation scholarship that will cover his entire education—through earning a doctorate degree. Maggie is considering Evergreen University in Olympia, Washington. James has earned a football scholarship that will cover his tuition at Portland State University (PSU). And Olivia is valedictorian of this year's graduating class and has been accepted in the honors program at PSU.

Roosevelt's graduating class participates in an annual ritual of marching through the hallways in their caps and gowns, as peers, teachers, and administrators cheer them on. The day is filled with lots of laughs and tearful goodbyes, as the graduates begin the next chapter of their lives.

The results of our week are available for on-demand viewing (at DigitalSkillsWorkshop.com). Our objective was to document our process with video in a manner that teachers elsewhere could replicate.

COMMON CORE STRATEGIES

College- and career-ready students are expected to do the following:

- Make strategic use of digital media (such as textual, graphical audio, visual, and interactive elements) in presentations to enhance understanding of findings, reasoning, and evidence, and to add interest.

Assign students to reflect on one of the films and documentaries viewed in class (or one of their own choosing) to prepare an in-class presentation about its strengths and weaknesses. Instruct them to use Keynote or PowerPoint, or a free online platform such as Prezi.com or Google Presentation. Establish a time limit that allows for audience questions and answers. For large classes have students present in groups, structured so that each member is accountable for a portion of the talk. Show TED Talks that feature young speakers (search online for TEDxYouth).

REFLECTIONS ON COLLABORATION

Collaborations between journalism schools and secondary educators, and between their students, can bolster broader adoption of journalistic learning strategies. In particular, such partnerships can support teachers who may otherwise be intimidated by new technology. College mentors also help to bridge generational gaps and can serve as positive role models for younger students.

Also, professional development does not have to be ineffective or boring. Video can be used in inventive ways to capture classroom experiences for online teaching and professional development.

TAKEAWAYS

Digital storytelling reinforces writing skills, adding the dimension of sight.

- Show short films and documentaries as examples of visual storytelling.
- Have students compare visual techniques with writing techniques.
- Encourage students to use storyboarding to organize their ideas before shooting.

Organize student teams and set them up for success.

- Break up cliques and close friends when assigning teams.
- Assign each group at least one tech-savvy student.
- Facilitate a story pitch session that empowers student-generated ideas.

Collaborate with journalism schools in your community to create mentorship programs.

- Identify faculty advisers or student media group leaders.
- Ask whether college mentors are eligible to receive credit as an extra benefit.
- Inquire about the school's ability to donate used gear.

RESOURCES

Free Technology Sources

Adopt A Classroom: www.adoptaclassroom.org

Donors Choose: www.donorschoose.org/teachers

Storyboard Templates: www.the-flying-animator.com/storyboard-template.html; www.educationworld.com/tools_templates/template_strybrd_8panels.doc

Conclusion
Looking to the Future

Knowledge emerges only through invention and re-invention, through the restless, impatient, continuing, hopeful inquiry human beings pursue in the world, with the world, and with each other.

—Freire, 1970, p. 72

In October 2014, Palo Alto High celebrated the grand opening of its new Media Arts Center, a two-story, state-of-the-art complex with technological facilities that rival those at many universities and professional media organizations. Esther Wojcicki abandoned her paltry portable classroom for a glass-enclosed room complete with smart boards and new furnishings. The center of the complex is an open atrium, allowing sunlight from every direction. Both levels are wired for cameras, lighting, and sound. There is a new video production studio, several computer labs, and a photojournalism lab. Flat-screen monitors beam in images from around the world as students scurry about practicing journalism.

Media icon Arianna Huffington and celebrity alumnus James Franco were among the luminaries who participated in the three-day celebration. Although I was thrilled to witness and participate in this new triumph and transformation of Palo Alto High's media program, I was also fearful about how its magnificence might be misinterpreted. My concern was that passive observers, reading or hearing about these grand facilities, might view the school's achievements as unobtainable. I also feared that other educators would be so intimidated, they would not even try.

There is no doubting the Palo Alto community's wealth. Yet as we demonstrated at Roosevelt High, there are creative ways to initiate change—even when funds are limited or it seems the odds are against you. Local universities and media organizations can be great resources for equipment and mentorship. It is significant to remember that Wojcicki began her program with little more than copies of the daily newspapers, and that she started with just 19 students. In many ways, Palo Alto High School's grand results emerged from a fundamental philosophical shift that occurred 25 years earlier. Wojcicki and her colleagues challenged conventions, as have other teachers whose successes are chronicled within these pages.

The school's new Media Arts Center was funded by a bond measure, overwhelmingly approved by voters just prior to the 2008 recession. Wojcicki, Kandell, and Austin spent 5 years crafting a compelling and well-researched proposal in the lead-up to their successful bid for financing (Kadvany, 2014). (Ellen Austin now teaches at the Harker School in San Jose, California.) They visited existing facilities and sought input from professionals. Not surprisingly, given the program's core philosophy, students played a significant role in the planning process.

Yet such efforts are more likely to succeed in affluent areas where residents enjoy more discretionary time and a high tax base. Affluent students leave the starting gate with significant advantages that cannot be ignored. Also, historical and structural forces are at play that make it more difficult for disenfranchised students to get ahead.

Although certain U.S. communities are undeniably more privileged than others, they may not be trouble-free. Competitive pressure runs high in communities and academic settings where many families aspire to have their sons and daughters enter the Ivy League. Although no scientific correlation has been established, high schools in the mid-peninsula area have experienced a high number of student suicides in recent years. The community responded by forming a task force, now known as Project Safety Net, to address the problem (PSN, 2014). Challenges can exist in all communities. Change comes with a willingness to face them head on. Educational reform cannot just be a campaign slogan. It thrives through a process of committed action.

OBSTACLES TO OVERCOME

Most will acknowledge that situated learning has merits. It is aligned with familiar pedagogical approaches that have been in and out of vogue throughout the history of American education, including project-based learning, inquiry-based learning, and progressive education. However, pushback often arises when discussing matters of standardization, assessment, and class size. As the argument goes, it is commonly accepted that mass education requires a massive "cookie-cutter" approach to teaching.

Consequently, in many parts of the United States, the educational experience is becoming more scripted (Au, 2011). Yet the real world that students will inherit does not work by formulaic principles. There are no dress rehearsals for the complexities of life and the uncertainties of the future. Students who are not taught to think are likely to suffer severe consequences—and, despite millions of dollars spent in legislative reform, will be left behind.

It is easy to blame teachers. Yet most are diligent, underpaid civil servants—constrained by a system that some suggest no longer values their professionalism. Teachers care, but often their hands are tied. Statistics reveal considerable hard truths. Over the past 15 years, teacher attrition has grown 50%. Teacher turnover is 16.8% and is higher than 20% in some urban communities. In some school districts the teacher dropout rate exceeds the student dropout rate (Kain, 2011). Yet the exodus is understandable, given that by many accounts public education is under siege as teachers bear the brunt of the criticisms associated with poor performance (Ravitch, 2010).

Censorship of student media in many parts of the United States remains another impediment. In *Hazelwood vs. Kuhlmeier* (1988), the Supreme Court ruled in favor of an administration's right to exercise prior restraint of school-sponsored expression. In that instance, a principal deemed that articles about divorce and teen pregnancy were inappropriate for publication the school paper. Such subjects are considered tame by today's standards. Yet the decision continues to have a chilling effect on student media across the nation.

The rise of the Internet has intensified the fears of school administrators who resist transparency and want to avoid criticism. Concerns relate to the new ease with which students can publish—online and via social media platforms.

Since 1974, the Student Press Law Center has worked diligently to inform educators about the merits of free expression. One of the advocacy group's compelling arguments asks administrators to consider which is better: providing students with adviser-guided opportunities to express their opinions in a responsible manner, or restricting school-sponsored expression in a way that forces it out into the unfettered spheres of social media, where it can be driven by rumor and innuendo.

Ellen Austin, who formerly taught at Palo Alto High, notes the irony of the Hazelwood decision: "Someone can be three doors down in social studies, studying Thomas Jefferson's principles of democracy and free speech, and then that same child could ostensibly in many states in this nation, try and write an article in the school paper using that free speech, and be suppressed by a government official."

Seven states, including Arkansas, California, Colorado, Iowa, Kansas, Massachusetts, and Oregon, have enacted "anti-Hazelwood" legislation designed to expand student speech (SPLC, 2012). There is also a mounting grassroots effort to overturn Hazelwood. In the interim, administrators who place heavy regulations on expression need to weigh the consequences of their actions. The risks include stifling creativity and the development of autonomy in students.

GOING FORWARD

The view that media arts, and more specifically journalism curricula, should become an essential component of secondary-level English courses has numerous advocates (Blanchard & Christ, 1993; Hart, 2001; Hobbs, 2007). However, a fundamental philosophical shift is required within the discipline of English language arts for journalistic learning to have a broader impact. Hobbs (2007) interprets this pedagogical shift as "restoring the medieval *trivium* of grammar, dialectic, and rhetoric as the center posts in English education," and further, that it will "help students situate themselves in their own culture and make the basic processes of language and communication fully available for students' use" (p. 7).

Austin says, "English teachers need to understand that journalism isn't 'something else'—it is English, being put to work." Journalism offers educators a vast repertoire of rhetorical resources that are readily available to enhance learning. Teachers who are demonstrating success must collectively commit to altering prevailing discourses that presently marginalize use of journalistic approaches in our schools.

Teacher training is one area for intervention. Preservice teachers come to the profession with fresh eyes and can greatly benefit from learning how to incorporate journalistic practices in their work with students. Professional development programs can introduce journalistic strategies to working teachers. However, both groups need ongoing support. Initiatives like our Digital Skills Workshop and a project called "Searchlights and Sunglasses" by Eric Newton, formerly of the Knight Foundation, arm teachers with new tools (see searchlightsandsunglasses.org). The Journalism Education Association also offers its members a robust set of teaching modules. All are available online.

The nation's top university-based journalism schools can also play an active role. Although their resources may also be strained, they have legions of sharp students who can support high school teachers and students within their communities. Such a strategy can effectively bridge the gap between college and high school, providing younger students with mentors who can serve as role models. These programs are envisioned as *reverse internships,* which can provide college students with opportunities to mentor as well as learn from their mentees.

In addition to Digital Skills Workshop at Roosevelt High in Portland, our research team has run successful after-school programs and summer camps in Eugene. In 2013, we piloted *Cascadia,* a citywide magazine created by students from four Eugene-area high schools. Now in its third year, students are mentored by University of Oregon undergraduates during weekly publication meetings held at our journalism school.

Working, retired, and laid-off journalists are also a great resource. Dorothy Gilliam became the first African American woman reporter at the *Washington Post* in 1961. Her legacy is *Prime Movers,* an after-school program that sends working journalists and college students into high schools in Washington, DC, and Philadelphia. Leslie Seifert, formerly an editor at *Newsday,* leads a similar mentorship program called *Journalists in Schools,* which aims to create student-driven news bureaus in high schools across New York City.

There is also a burgeoning *news literacy* movement taking shape, through a partnership between numerous mainstream media organizations and foundations. In fall 2014 a workgroup funded by the Poynter Institute and McCormick Foundation convened in Chicago and put forth a clear and distinct set of recommendations for ushering in change, all of which are very much aligned with the principles and strategies articulated throughout this book:

- We recommend teachers be empowered to teach news literacy with professional development plus easy access to news literacy toolkits and online resources and we think a central repository for news literacy resources could be helpful.
- We also recommend news literacy education be incorporated into teachers' colleges' curricula so that newly trained teachers are empowered to teach news literacy.
- We recommend that those who are teaching news literacy be encouraged to write about their classroom experiences and best practices for audiences of educators and the general public, including via Op-Ed pieces, to help inform other educators, school administrators, education policymakers, and the public about news literacy education.
- We recommend that those striving to spread news literacy education seek to engage classroom teachers as well as school,

district, and state administrators and national education policy-makers—so both a grassroots approach and a top-down approach to make news literacy education more widely available.

- To help engage and incentivize teachers and administrators to incorporate news literacy education, we recommend that a document be created that maps Common Core standards to news literacy educational opportunities.
- We recommend stronger partnerships among news literacy educators with student media, including student journalists and teachers who are student newspaper and student media advisors.
- We further recommend more outreach from universities that have journalism departments and programs both beyond their majors and into nearby schools and communities to help make news literacy education available to expanding audiences.
- For community colleges, we recommend providing news literacy classes that can result in senior college credit through articulation agreements that recognize the value of news literacy education.
- We also recommend bringing journalists to classrooms and, where possible, students to newsrooms/news organizations, so students can learn more about professional news reporting.
- We recommend looking to cyber-bullying educational programs as another place that might be a vehicle for news literacy education because students can be instructed in the rights and responsibilities that accompany their activities as publishers, including their social media participation, which would help encourage positive civic engagement. (Rosenberg-Belton, 2014)

TAKE ACTION

Committed individuals are at the core of successful programs and strategies chronicled in this book—people who exhibit courage and unceasing conviction. These are teachers who learned to trust their students and to trust themselves. They were willing to step outside the confines of the status quo, recognizing that breaking ground requires relentless effort.

Esther Wojcicki and her colleagues want their new Media Arts Center to serve as a beacon of inspiration—pointing toward the future of what is possible in education. Although Palo Alto students and faculty will experience its immediate benefits, a greater vision is to have the Center become a global hub and laboratory for the development of tomorrow's curricula and practices. Paly's media faculty invites teachers, administrators,

researchers, journalists, and anyone committed to the cause to participate. A key priority is addressing the needs of underserved and diverse
communities across the nation.

Research can inform and inspire change, but real transformation requires committed action. One of the major impediments to real reform
in education is complacency—an unwillingness to challenge conventional
thinking. Educational change often becomes a disingenuous campaign
slogan touted every election cycle—rather than a serious commitment to
alter the status quo.

It is not uncommon to have strong beliefs about how to "fix" education, based on our own experiences as products of the system. Yet we can
forget that our point of reference is the past. Consequently, we support
politicians and policies that perpetuate a vicious cycle, resulting in more
of the same. A memorable quote, often attributed to Albert Einstein,
states "insanity is doing the same thing over and over again and expecting
different results." Innovation requires a willingness to abandon the past
and to explore possibilities that may seem antithetical to what is familiar.

There are no panaceas that will magically "fix" education overnight—
or over the next decade. Yet there is much to learn from teachers who are
making a difference. It is perhaps no accident that Palo Alto is the birth-
place of much of the innovation we now celebrate in America. The Silicon
Valley is home to Google, Apple, Facebook, and numerous companies
with bright approaches to thinking that are transforming our economy
and the world. When you visit these companies' workspaces, you will not
find groups of people operating in silos or see very many in corner offices.
Rather, teams collaborate in open spaces and are committed to challenging the boundaries of conventional thinking—and many resemble newsrooms.

The examples described here demonstrate the value of real-world experiences to students' educational experiences, and to their development
of autonomy and a positive sense of self. In addition, these young people
have a contribution to make as they enter adulthood as citizens, professionals, and stakeholders in the evolution of our democracy. When students are empowered and know that their voice matters, they do not drop
out—they dig in and commit to playing a vital role in shaping the future.

Journalistic Learning Study

The intent of this study was to discover whether the qualitative findings at Palo Alto High School were more than anecdotal, through quantitative analysis of a significantly larger sample of high school students from a variety of locales.

Self-determination Theory (Deci & Ryan, 1985, 2000) and the *situated learning* (Lave & Wenger, 1991) and *communities-of-practice* (Wenger, 1998) constructs provided appropriate theoretical frameworks for this 2012 national quantitative survey that looked at journalistic learning's effect on motivation, learning strategies, and personal growth.

RESEARCH QUESTIONS

Three proposed quantitative questions were derived from the literature and sought to draw comparisons and provide new insights about the effectiveness of various forms of English language arts instruction.

Key areas of the literature relate to the significance of intrinsic motivation and meeting students' basic psychological needs, which Deci and Ryan (1985, 2000) argue are dependent on three factors: autonomy, competency, relatedness. Therefore, the first research question explores students' self-perceptions about these areas. Additionally, it addresses how students approach their various forms of language arts studies in terms of learning styles and strategies. It looks at possible tactics students may employ when preparing to fulfill an assignment or take a test in journalism versus other language arts courses. It also explores matters pertaining to the "digital divide," a term associated with previous data that suggests certain student populations lack access—not only to new technology but to the skills necessary to make effective use of new technology (Compaine, 2001; Norris, 2001).

R1—Is there a difference between high school journalism students and other language arts students in self-reported motivational beliefs and learning strategies, after controlling for school and student demographics (community type, class-standing, or socioeconomic status)?

The second research question addresses personal growth and identity construction. Specifically, it pertains to how journalism courses may offer student participants a venue for negotiating who they are, how they "fit in," and where they "belong"—within various social strata. This process occurs during a critical period of adolescent development (Coleman, 1974; Steinberg & Silverberg, 1986).

R2—Is there a difference between how high school journalism students and other language arts students self-report their personal growth and sense of self?

The final quantitative research question seeks to identify why students self-select certain language arts courses over others. Obviously, some are required, others are recommended, and yet others are chosen as electives. The question explores what motivates students' selections, as well as their perceptions about related benefits.

R3—Why do high school students enroll in journalism, and what short-term and long-term benefits do they perceive?

PARTICIPANTS

Approximately 20 U.S. high schools were approached to have their students participate in the study's anonymous survey. To balance the sample, journalism instructors who agreed to participate were asked to recruit colleagues in their general English departments. This was to provide a sufficient representation of Advanced Placement English, honors, and general English students in the survey pool.

All are categories of ELA courses, with specific distinctions. Although general English courses are required, journalism and Advanced Placement courses are self-selected. The intent of the survey was to investigate what motivates students to make these curricular choices and their perceptions about the benefits associated with either selection.

To assess participants' socioeconomic status, they were asked about access to broadband, computers at home, and the number of individuals who shared the computer at home. In addition, students were asked about part-time employment and how they traveled to school.

The survey targeted both high school juniors and seniors. However, given that many classes include mixed grade levels, freshmen and sophomores were permitted to participate and were included in the analysis. All participating students had to provide written parental consent. No form of compensation, either monetary or course credit, was offered to students or their teachers. All research was compliant with University of Oregon Institutional Review Board procedures. Administrators and teachers authorized the inclusion of their schools and references to classroom and field assignment activities.

RESPONDENT PROFILE

In total 664 high school students took the survey, representing 10 different schools across the United States, from the 20 approached. Table A.1 provides a breakdown of the percentage portion of the total sample represented by each school that participated in the study.

The balance in socioeconomic composition among the participants was as follows: high 342 (51%) and medium 320 (49%). As shown in Table A.1, Palo Alto High School students represented 168 (25%) of the total survey sample, and of those Palo Alto High students 88 (52%) chose to report on journalism, versus 80 (48%) nonjournalism. Data from

Table A.1. School Geographic Locations

City/School	Respondents	Percentage	SES
Palo Alto High School	168	25%	High
Palo Alto, CA School #2	140	21%	High
Annandale, VA	34	5.1%	High
East Palo Alto, CA School	67	10%	Medium
East Bakersfield, CA	19	2.9%	Medium
Sacramento, CA	163	24.6%	Medium
Stockton, CA	19	2.9%	Medium
Iowa City, IA	47	7.1%	Medium
Eugene, OR	3	0.5%	Medium
Newark, NJ	2	0.3%	Medium

High SES = $100k+ annual household income; median SES = $40k to $99k annual household income. Source: U.S. Census data.

two students were removed because they entered inaccurate school code information, effectively reducing the sample to 662.

Table A.2 shows the grade-level breakdown for participants was Seniors (n = 227, 34.3%), Juniors (n = 152, 23%), Sophomores (n = 150, 22.7%), and Freshmen (n = 133, 20.1%). Students reported their ethnicity as Caucasian (n = 336, 50.8%), African American, (n = 20, 3%), Asian American (n = 151, 22%), Hispanic (n = 92, 13.9%), and Other (n = 63, 9.5%).

As shown in Table A.3, community types were self-reported as Urban (n = 104, 15.7%), Suburban (n = 552, 83.4%), Rural (n = 3, .5%), and Other (n = 3, .5%). In terms of gender, more than half were females (n = 393, 59.4%), compared to the males (n = 269, 40.6%).

ACADEMIC PROFILE

In terms of academics, it was clear that students might have taken a varied mix of ELA courses. Therefore, participants were instructed to pick an area of study to reflect on for all of the remaining survey questions, from a list that included English, Journalism, AP Language and Composition, AP Literature and Composition, International Baccalaureate Program, and Honors English. As shown in Table A.4, of the respondents 253 (38.3%) chose general English, 190 (28.7%) Journalism, 36 (5.4%) AP Language and Composition, 100 (15.1%) AP Literature and Composition, 82 (12.4%) Honors English, and only 1 (2%) International Baccalaureate Program.

Table A.2. Class Standing Breakdown (N = 662)

Class Level	Number	Percentage
Senior	227	34.3%
Junior	152	23.0%
Sophomore	150	22.7%
Freshmen	133	20.1%

Table A.3. Community Type Breakdown (N = 662)

Community Type	Number	Percentage
Urban	104	15.7%
Suburban	552	83.4%
Rural	3	0.5%
Other	3	0.5%
No Response	1	0.2%

Table A.4. Academic Profile (n = 662)

Course Type	Number	Percentage
General English	253	38.3%
Journalism	190	28.7%
AP Language & Composition	36	5.4%
AP Literature & Composition	100	15.1%
Honors English	82	12.4%
International Baccalaureate	1	2%

Therefore, the breakdown was journalism students 190 (28.7%) compared to nonjournalism 472 (71.3%).

SUMMARY OF FINDINGS

Findings related to Research Question 1 revealed that social-situated learning, intrinsic motivation, and skill enhancement were rated higher by journalism students than by nonjournalism students, after controlling for school and student demographics (community type, class standing, or socioeconomic status).

Journalism students in less affluent communities report motivational beliefs and learning strategies that are similar to students in affluent communities. This challenges the notion that the success of the Palo Alto program is an anomaly. Further, class standing was a significant factor in how journalism students self-reported motivational beliefs and learning strategies. Seniority in a journalism program was associated with higher ratings.

Findings related to Research Question 2 indicated that journalism students report significantly higher levels of personal growth and sense of self than nonjournalism students. Finally, findings related to Research Question 3 provided several useful comparisons about why students enroll in journalism, given its status as an elective. On the open-ended responses, journalism students were far more likely than AP English literature students to say they enrolled in their course for enjoyment/fulfillment. Both journalism students and AP Literature students believe their respective courses will enhance their skills. However, AP Literature students were more inclined to enroll with that intention in mind, as compared with journalism students. Therefore, although skill enhancement is important to both groups, journalism students view their course path as a preferable way to accomplish that goal.

In the "true" versus "false" responses, journalism students were equally likely to view their course as being beneficial to future coursework as AP Literature students and that their respective courses were in line with their academic interests. However, journalism students were more likely than AP Literature students to assert that their course was in line with their personal interests. Both journalism and AP Literature students believe their respective courses will look good on their transcripts to prospective colleges.

Other key findings relate to social-situated learning. Journalism students were significantly more likely than AP Literature students to report that their course was structured around teamwork. Additionally, there is a substantial difference in the amount of coursework being published in journalism classes when compared with AP Literature classes.

All told, the journalism students surveyed in this study are more intrinsically motivated to take journalism than nonjournalism students who take other forms of language arts. Although both groups believe their choices will "look good" to prospective colleges, journalism students seek personal fulfillment from their classes over extrinsic rewards.

Resources

Check NewsworthyBook.com for new and updated lists of resources.

2013 AP Stylebook Quick Quizzes: grammar.about.com/b/2013/07/24/a-quick-quiz-from-the-2013-ap-stylebook.htm

American Society of Newspaper Editors' SchoolJournalism.org (resources for high school journalists): www.schooljournalism.org

EditTeach.org (resources for journalism instructors at many levels: high school, college, newsroom, etc.): www.editteach.org

The Good, the Bad & the Ugly, or Why It's a Good Idea to Evaluate Web Resources (by Susan E. Beck of the New Mexico State University Library): lib.nmsu.edu/instruction/eval.html

Journalism Education Association: jea.org; curriculum.jea.org

Journalists in Schools: journalistsinschools.org

JPROF.com (resources for college journalism instructors): www.jprof.com

National Scholastic Press Association Student Sourcebook (a directory of links and contact information for resources and organizations of interest to high school journalists): studentpress.journ.umn.edu/nspa/

Newsroom 101 (grammar and journalistic style): newsroom101.net

No Train, No Gain (a collection of handouts and contacts for newsroom training): www.notrain-nogain.org

Rethinking Schools: Online Geography Test (a good quiz to give young reporters): www.rethinkingschools.org/just_fun/games/mapgame.html

Society of Professional Journalists—Journalist's Toolbox: www.journaliststoolbox.org/archive/teaching-tools/

The News Literacy Project: www.thenewsliteracyproject.org

Thsrs: The Shorter Thesaurus (a great tool for headline writing): www.ironicsans.com/thsrs/

Tolerance.org (teaching Title IX and gender equity): www.tolerance.org

Verification Junkie (a fact-checking tool from Josh Stearns that centralizes several social media verification tools in one place): verificationjunkie.com

References

Alliance for Excellent Education. (2012). Available at all4ed. org/?s=&category=high-school-dropout-rates&show_only=press&current-page=6

American Press Institute (2015). How millennials get news: Inside the habits of America's first digital generation. Available at www.americanpressinstitute. org/publications/reports/survey-research/millennials-news/

ASNE (American Society of News Editors). (1978). Report of the ASNE Committee on minorities, Columbia, MO: ASNE. Available at asne.org/content. asp?pl=28&sl=15&contentid=57

ASNE (American Society of News Editors). (2011). Newsroom census. Columbia, MO: ASNE.

ASNE (American Society of News Editors). (2012). Newsroom employment up slightly, minority number plunge for the third year. Columbia, MO: ASNE.

Au, W. (2011). Teaching under the new Taylorism: High-stakes testing and the standardization of the 21st century curriculum. *Journal of Curriculum Studies, 43*(1), 25–45.

Ayscue, J. B., & Orfield, G. (2014). School district lines stratify educational opportunity by race and poverty. *Race and Social Problems, 7*(1), 5–30.

Ball, S. J. (1990). *Foucault and education: Disciplines and knowledge.* London: Routledge.

Beghetto, R. A. (2009). The search for the unexpected: Finding creativity in the micromoments of the classroom. *Psychology of Aesthetics, Creativity, and the Arts, 3,* 2–5.

Biemiller, L. (1986). Asian students fear top colleges use quota systems. *Chronicle of Higher Education, 33*(12), 1, 34–36.

Blanchard, R. O., & Christ, W. G. (1993). *Media education and the liberal arts: A blueprint for the new professionalism.* Hillsdale, NJ: Lawrence Erlbaum Associates.

Blinn, J. R. (1982). *A comparison of selected writing skills of high school journalism and non-journalism students.* Available at search.proquest.com/docview/3032 44941?accountid=14698

Bowen, C. P. (2014, November 21). Journalism may be Common Core's new English MediaShift. Available at www.pbs.org/mediashift/2014/10/journalism-may-be-common-cores-new-english/

Brass, J. J. (2008). Local knowledge and digital movie composing in an after-school literacy program. *Journal of Adolescent & Adult Literacy, 51*(6), 464–473.

Bridgeland, J. (2006). *The silent epidemic: Perspectives of high school dropouts.* Available at eric.ed.gov/?id=ED513444

Bruner, J. S. (1961). The art of discovery. *Harvard Educational Review, 31,* 21–32.

Carter, P. (2006). Straddling Boundaries: Identity, Culture, and School. *Sociology of Education, 79*(4), 304–328.

Castro, J. R., & Rice, K. G. (2003). Perfectionism and ethnicity: Implications for depressive symptoms and self-reported academic achievement. *Cultural diversity and ethnic minority psychology, 9*(1), 64–78.

Chang, E. C. (1998). Cultural differences, perfectionism, and suicidal risk in a college population: Does social problem solving still matter? *Cognitive Therapy and Research, 22*(3), 237–254.

Chua, A. (2007). *Day of empire: How hyperpowers rise to global dominance and why they fall.* New York: Doubleday.

Clark, R. (2006). *Writing tools: 50 essential strategies for every writer* (1st ed.). New York, NY: Little, Brown, and Co.

Cohen, D. K., & Hill, H. C. (1998). State policy and classroom performance: Mathematics reform in California, *CPRE Policy Briefs* (RB-23-May). Philadelphia, PA: Consortium for Policy Research in Education (CPRE), Graduate School of Education, University of Pennsylvania.

Cohen, D. K., & Hill, H. C. (2000). Instructional policy and classroom performance: The mathematics reform in California. *Teachers College Record, 102*(2), 294–343.

Coleman, D. (2011). Bringing the Common Core to life. Transcript. Available at usny.nysed.gov/rttt/docs/bringingthecommoncoretolife/part4transcript.pdf

Coleman, J. C. (1974). *Relationships in adolescence.* London, UK: Routledge and Kegan Paul.

Common Core State Standards Initiative (CCSS). (2010). English language arts standards: Introduction—Key considerations. Available at www.corestandards.org/ELA-Literacy/introduction/key-design-consideration/

Compaine, B. M. (Ed.). (2001). *The digital divide: Facing a crisis or creating a myth?* Cambridge, MA: The MIT Press.

Costa, P. T., Jr., Zonderman, A. B., & McCrae R. R. (1985). Longitudinal course of social support in adulthood and old age. In I. G. Sarason & B. R. Sarason

(Eds.), *Social support: Theory, research, and applications* (pp. 137–154). Dordrecht, The Netherlands: Martinus Nijhoff.

Crenshaw, K. (1989). Demarginalizing the intersection of race and sex: A black feminist critique of antidiscrimination doctrine, feminist theory and antiracist politics. *University of Chicago Legal Forum, 139.*

CSPA (Columbia Scholastic Press Association). (2014). 2014—Awards for Student Work Gold Circle Awards—Collegiate Recipients. Available at cspa. columbia.edu/recepient-lists/2014-awards-student-work-gold-circle-awards-collegiate-recipients

CSPA (Columbia Scholastic Press Association). (2015). *2015—Awards for Student Work Gold Circle Awards—Collegiate Recipients.* Available at cspa.columbia. edu/recepient-lists/2015-awards-student-work-gold-circle-awards-collegiate-recipients

Cuban, L. (1993). *How teachers taught: Constancy and change in American classrooms 1890–1990* (2nd ed.). New York, NY: Teachers College Press.

Cummins, J. (2001). Empowering minority students: A framework for intervention. *Harvard Educational Review, 71*(4), 649–675.

Cutler, K. (2015, January 10). East of Palo Alto's Eden: Race and the formation of Silicon Valley. TechCrunch. Available at techcrunch.com/2015/01/10/east-of-palo-altos-eden/

Deci, E. L., & Ryan, R. M. (1985). *Intrinsic motivation and self-determination in human behavior.* New York, NY: Plenum.

Deci, E. L., & Ryan, R. M. (2000). The "what" and "why" of goal pursuits: Human needs and the self-determination of behavior. *Psychological Inquiry, 11,* 227–268.

Deci, E. L., & Ryan, R. M. (2002). *Handbook of self-determination research.* Rochester, NY: University of Rochester Press.

Dewey, J. (1997). *Experience and education.* New York, NY: Macmillan. (Original work published 1938)

Diamandis, P. (2014, December 8). Mobile is eating the world. Available at www. linkedin.com/pulse/20141208193320-994365-mobile-is-eating-the-world

Dvorak, J. (1988, Summer). High school publications experience as a factor in college-level writing. *Journalism Quarterly, 65*(2), 392–398.

Dvorak, J. (1998). Journalism student performance on advanced placement exams. *Journalism & Mass Communication Educator, 53*(3), 4–12.

Dvorak, J., Bowen, C. P., & Choi, C. (2009, January 1). Minority journalism student academic comparisons between those with and those without high school print media experience. *Journalism & Mass Communication Educator, 64*(3), 258–272.

Dvorak, J., & Choi, C. (2009, January 1). High school journalism, academic performance correlate. *Newspaper Research Journal, 30*(3), 75–89.

Ed-Data. (2014). California Department of Education. Available at www.ed-data.k12.ca.us/App_Resx/EdDataClassic/fsTwoPanel.aspx?#!bottom=/_layouts/EdDataClassic/profile.asp?tab=1&level=07&ReportNumber=16&County=43&fyr=1314&District=69641&School=4335782

Elbow, P. (1973). *Writing without teachers.* New York, NY: Oxford University Press.

Farber, D. A. (2003). *The First Amendment.* New York, NY: Foundation Press.

Farrell, E. F. (2005) Among freshmen, a growing digital divide. *The Chronicle of Higher Education, 51*(22), A32.

Fischer, C. S. (1996). *Inequality by design: Cracking the bell curve myth.* Princeton, NJ: Princeton University Press.

Fishkin, S. F. (1985). *From fact to fiction: Journalism & imaginative writing in America.* Baltimore, MD: Johns Hopkins University Press.

Fordham, S., & Ogbu, J. (1986). Black students' school success: Coping with the burden of "acting white." *Urban Review, 18,* 176–206.

Foucault, M. (1984). *The order of discourse.* In M. Shapiro (Ed.), *Language and politics* (pp. 108–138). Oxford: Blackwell.

Fox, S. (2007). Latinos Online. Pew Internet and American Life Project. Available at www.pewhispanic.org/2009/12/22/latinos-online-2006-2008-narrowing-the-gap/

Freire, P. (1970). *Pedagogy of the oppressed.* New York, NY: Continuum.

Glinberg, S. (2013, September 9). Help a student: Donate your iPad, iPhone or iPod Touch. Available at kidcalc.wordpress.com/2010/06/15/recycle-your-iphone-or-ipod-touch/

Goins, M. (2008). Reflections on the shame of the nation: The restoration of apartheid schools in America. *Ohio State Law Journal, 69,* 1085–1087.

Goode, J. (2010). Mind the gap: The digital dimension of college access. *The Journal of Higher Education, 81*(5), 583–618.

Greenberg, M. A., Wortman, C. B., & Stone, A. A. (1996). Emotional expression and physical health: Revising traumatic memories or fostering self-regulation? *Journal of Personality and Social Psychology, 71,* 588–602.

Gross, J. J. (1998). Antecedent- and response-focused emotion regulation: Divergent consequences for experience, expression, and physiology. *Journal of Personality and Social Psychology, 74,* 224–237.

Guskey, T. R. (2002). Professional development and teacher change. *Teachers and Teaching: Theory and practice, 8*(3), 381–391.

Harrower, T. (2013). *Inside reporting: A practical guide to the craft of journalism* (3rd ed.). New York, NY: McGraw-Hill.

Hart, A. (2001, March 1). Awkward practice: Teaching media in English. *Changing English, 8*(1), 65–81.

Hauser, B. (2011). *The new kids: Big dreams and brave journeys at a high school for immigrant teens.* New York, NY: Free Press.

Herrnstein, R. J., & Murray, C. A. (1994). *The bell curve: Intelligence and class structure in American life*. New York, NY: Free Press.

Hess, D., & Posselt, J. (2002). How high school students experience and learn from the discussion of controversial public issues. *Journal of Curriculum and Supervision, 17*(4), 283–314.

Hobbs, R. (2007). *Reading the media: Media literacy in high school English*. New York, NY: Teachers College Press.

Hull, G. A., & Katz, M. L. (2006). Crafting an agentive self: Case studies of digital storytelling. *Research in the Teaching of English, 41*(1), 43–81.

Jacobs, E. (2011). Re(place) your typical writing assignment: An argument for place-based writing. *English Journal, 100*(3), 49–54.

Jenkins, H. (2009). *Confronting the challenges of participatory culture: Media education for the 21st century*. Cambridge, MA: MIT Press.

Kadvany, E. (2014, October 17). Palo Alto school-district bond, dreams of students brought media center to life. Palo Alto Online. Available at www.palo-altoonline.com/news/2014/10/17/a-media-center-for-the-next-century

Kain, E. (2011, March 8). High teacher turnover rates are a big problem for America's public schools. Forbes.com. Available at www.forbes.com/sites/erikkain/2011/03/08/high-teacher-turnover-rates-are-a-big-problem-for-americas-public-schools/

Kennedy, M. (1998). Form and substance in teacher inservice education, *Research Monograph No. 13*. Madison, WI: National Institute for Science Education, University of Wisconsin–Madison.

Kiemer, K., Groschner, A., Pehmer, A. K., & Seidel, T. (2015). Effects of a classroom discourse intervention on teachers' practice and students' motivation to learn mathematics and science. *Learning and Instruction, 35*, 94–103.

Kohut, A. (2013, October 7). Pew surveys of audience habits suggest perilous future for news. Poynter. Available at www.poynter.org/latest-news/top-stories/225139/pew-surveys-of-audience-habits-suggest-perilous-future-for-news/

Kosar, K. R. (2011). *Ronald Reagan and education policy*. Boulder, CO, Washington, DC: Studies in Governance and Politics.

Ladson-Billings, G. (1994). *The dreamkeepers: Successful teachers of African American children* (1st ed., Jossey-Bass education series). San Francisco, CA: Jossey-Bass.

Lambert, J. (2007). Digital storytelling. *Futurist, 41*(2), 25.

Lave, J., & Wenger, E. (1991). *Situated learning: Legitimate peripheral participation*. Cambridge, UK: Cambridge University Press.

Lawrence, S., & Shapiro, G. (2010). Crime trends in the city of East Palo Alto. UC Berkeley School of Law. Available at www.law.berkeley.edu/files/EPA_Main_Report_Final.pdf

Leary, M. R., & Tangney, J. P. (2003). *Handbook of self and identity.* New York, NY: Guilford Press.

Lee, S. (1994). Behind the model-minority stereotype: Voices of high- and low-achieving Asian American students. *Anthropology & Education Quarterly, 25*(4), 413–429.

Madison, E. (2012). *Journalistic learning: Rethinking and redefining language arts curricula.* Available at earch.proquest.com/docview/1237275104?acc ountid=14698

McGill, L. T. (2000). *Newsroom diversity: Meeting the challenge.* Arlington, VA: Freedom Forum.

McLaren, P., & Leonard, P. (1993). *Paulo Freire: A critical encounter.* London: Routledge.

McMahon, T. (2012). Challenging students to move outside their peer group cliques. Available at ojs.great-ideas.org/index.php/ENC/article/view/854

Mehan, H. (1979). *Learning lessons: Social organization in the classroom.* Cambridge, MA: Harvard University Press.

Melton, K. (January 21, 2010). What will be the fate of my high school? Oregonlive.com. Available at www.oregonlive.com/portland/index.ssf/2010/01/what_will_be_the_fate_of_my_hi.html

Morrell, E. (2004). *Linking literacy and popular culture: Finding connections for lifelong learning.* Norwood, MA: Christopher-Gordon.

Morris, J. (2009). *Troubling the waters: Fulfilling the promise of quality public schooling for black children.* New York, NY: Teachers College Press.

Moynahan, M. (2012, 14 October). Nicholas Lemann: Journalism is doing just fine. The Daily Beast. Available at www.thedailybeast.com/articles/2012/10/14/nicholas-lemann-journalism-is-doing-just-fine.html

NAEP (National Assessment of Educational Progress). (2011). Available at nces. ed.gov/nationsreportcard/studies/gaps/

NAMLE (National Association for Media Literacy Education). (2015). Media literary defined. Available at namle.net/publications/media-literacy-definitions/

Newton, E. (2013). Searchlights and sunglasses, James S. and James L. Knight Foundation and Reynolds Journalism Institute. Available at archive.org/stream/SearchlightsAndSunglassesEricNewton/Searchlights-and-Sunglasses_djvu.txt

Nichols, S. (2014, October 23). Journalism education and the 4 Cs of skills-based standards. MediaShift. Available at www.pbs.org/mediashift/2014/10/journalism-education-and-the-4-cs-of-skills-based-standards/

Norris, P. (2001). *Digital divide: Civic engagement, information poverty and the Internet world-wide.* Cambridge, MA: Cambridge University Press.

Oakes, J., & Lipton, M. (2007). *Teaching to change the world* (3rd ed.). Boston, MA: McGraw-Hill.

Palfrey, J. & Gasser. U. (2008). *Born digital: Understanding the first generation of digital natives.* New York, NY: Basic Books.

Palo Alto Unified School District. (2012). School accountability report cards. Available at www.pausd.org/community/about/sar.shtml

Papper, B. (2014). Radio Television Digital News Association (RTDNA) and Hofstra University Survey. Available at www.rtdna.org/pages/media_items/about-rtdnas-diversity-data491.php?id=491

Parks, C. (2014, June 12). Graduation 2014: At Roosevelt high school, a celebration, but also grieving. Oregonlive.com. Available at www.oregonlive.com/portland/index.ssf/2014/06/at_roosevelt_high_school_gradu.html

Pearl, A., & Knight, T. (1999). The democratic classroom: Theory to inform practice. Cresskill, NJ: Hampton Press.

Pennebaker, J. W. (1989). Confession, inhibition and disease. In L. Berkowitz (Ed.), *Advances in experimental social psychology* (Vol. 22, pp. 211–244). Orlando, FL: Academic Press.

Pew Internet Research. (2005). Teen content creators and consumers. Available at www.pewinternet.org/Reports/2005/Teen-Content-Creators-and-Consumers.aspx

Pew Internet and American Life Project. (2007) Demographics of Internet users. Available at www.pewinternet.org/trends/User_Demo_6.15.07.htm

Pew Internet Research. (2010). Content creation: Sharing, remixing, blogging, and more. Available at www.pewinternet.org/2010/02/03/part-3-social-media/#fn-479-13

Pew Research Center. (2012). The rise of intermarriage. Available at www.pew-socialtrends.org/2012/02/16/the-rise-of-intermarriage/

Pew Internet Research. (2013). Teens and technology 2013. Available at www.pewinternet.org/2013/03/13/teens-and-technology-2013/

Poindexter, P. (2012). *Millennials, news, and social media: Is news engagement a thing of the past?* New York, NY: Peter Lang.

Prensky, M. (2001). Digital natives, digital immigrants. *On the Horizon, 9*(5), 1–6.

PSN. (2014). Project Safety Net: Community Coalition. Available at www.psn-paloalto.com/about-us/community-coalition/

Ravitch, D. (2010). *The death and life of the great American school system: How testing and choice are undermining education.* New York, NY: Basic Books.

Reeve, J., & Lee, W. (2014). Students' classroom engagement produces longitudinal changes in classroom motivation. *Journal of Educational Psychology, 106*, 527–540.

Reimold, D. (2014, September 17). University of Oregon students embrace iPad-only publication, challenge traditional storytelling methods. Poytner.org. Available at www.poynter.org/how-tos/journalism-education/223274/university-of-oregon-students-embrace-ipad-only-publication-challenge-traditional-storytelling-methods/

Rivas-Rodriguez, M. (2004). Minority journalists' perceptions of the impact of minority executives. *Howard Journal of Communications, 15*(1), 39–55.

Rodgers, E. M. (2004). Interactions that scaffold reading performance. *Journal of Literacy Research, 36*(4), 501–532.

Rodriguez, R. (2003). *Brown: The last discovery of America.* New York NY: Penguin.

Rosenberg-Belton, G. (2014). Poynter Institute and McCormick Foundation workgroup session notes. (Unpublished)

Routman, R. (2005). *Writing essentials: Raising expectations and results while simplifying teaching.* Portsmouth, NH: Heinemann.

Ryan, R. M., & Deci, E. L. (2000). Self-determination theory and the facilitation of intrinsic motivation, social development, and well-being. *American Psychologist, 55,* 68–78.

Schwab, J. (1960). Enquiry, the science teacher, and the educator. *The Science Teacher, 27,* 6–11.

Schwartz, S., Côté, J., & Arnett, J. (January 1, 2005). Identity and agency in emerging adulthood. *Youth & Society, 37*(2), 201–229.

Schwartz, S. J., Luyckx, K., & Vignoles, V. L. (2011). *Handbook of identity theory and research.* New York, NY: Springer.

Seelye, K. Q. (2012, October 4). 4 Decades after clashes, Boston again debates school busing. *New York Times,* Available at www.nytimes.com/2012/10/05/education/new-boston-busing-debate-4-decades-after-fervid-clashes.html

Short, K. G., & Kauffman, G. (2000). Exploring sign systems within an inquiry system. In M. A. Gallego & S. Hollingsworth (Eds.), *What counts as literacy: Challenging the school standard* (pp. 42–61). New York, NY: Teachers College Press.

Siegler, M. (2010, August 4). Eric Schmidt: Every 2 days we create techcrunch.com/2010/08/04/schmidt-data/

Slotnik, D. (2012, February 8). Do Asian-Americans face bias in admissions at elite colleges? *New York Times.* Available at thechoice.blogs.nytimes.com/2012/02/08/do-asian-americans-face-bias-in-admissions-at-elite-colleges/

SPLC. (2012). Student Press Law Center. Available at www.splc.org/page/about

Steinberg, L., & Silverberg, S. B. (1986). The vicissitudes of autonomy in early adolescence. *Child Development, 57,* 841–851.

Sue, S., & Okazaki, S. (1990). Asian-American educational achievements. *American Psychologist, 45*(8), 913–920.

Tate, C. D., & Taylor, S. (2014). *Scholastic journalism.* Walden, MA: Wiley.

Thompson, L. (2011, October 4). 'Glee' Recap: Asian F. *Baltimore Sun.* Available at articles.baltimoresun.com/2011-10-04/entertainment/bal-glee-recap-20111004_1_glee-recap-glee-club-glee-cast

Tyson, K., Darity, W., Jr., & Castellino, D. R. (2005). It's not "a black thing": Understanding the burden of acting white and other dilemmas of higher achievement. *American Sociological Review, 70*(4), 582–605.

U.S. Census Bureau. (2010). www.census.gov/2010census/

U.S. Department of Commerce, National Telecommunications and Information Administration. (NTIA). (1995). Falling through the net: A survey of the "have nots" in rural and urban America. Available at www.ntia.doc.gov/ntiahome/fallingthru.html

U.S. Department of Commerce, National Telecommunications and Information Administration. (NTIA). (1998). Falling through the net II: New data on the digital divide. Available at www.ntia.doc.gov/ntiahome/net2

U.S. Department of Commerce, National Telecommunications and Information Administration. (1999). *Falling through the net: Defining the digital divide.* Available at www.ntia.doc.gov/report/1999/falling-through-net-defining-digital-divide

U.S. Department of Commerce, National Telecommunications and Information Administration. (2000). *Falling through the net: Toward digital inclusion.* Available at www.ntia.doc.gov/report/2000/falling-through-net-toward-digital-inclusion

van der Kolk, B. A., & van der Hart, O. (1991). The intrusive past: The flexibility of memory and the engraving of trauma. *American Imago, 48,* 424–454.

Villegas, A. M., & Lucas, T. (2002). Preparing culturally responsive teachers: Rethinking the curriculum. *Journal of Teacher Education, 53*(1), 20–32.

Vygotsky, L. S. (1987). Thinking and speech. In L. S. Vygotsky, *Collected works* (Vol. 1, pp. 39–285) (R. Rieber & A. Carton, Eds.; N. Minick, Trans.). New York, NY: Plenum. (Original works published 1934, 1960)

Wang, Y. L., Frechtling, J. A., & Sanders, W. L. (1999) *Exploring linkages between professional development and student learning: A pilot study.* Paper presented at the Annual Meeting of the American Educational Research Association, Montreal, April 1999.

WCBS-TV. (2010, December 15). Study shows sharp decline in East Palo Alto crime. Available at sanfrancisco.cbslocal.com/2010/12/15/study-shows-sharp-decline-in-east-palo-alto-crime/

Weinstein, N., & Hodgins, H. S. (2009). The moderating role of autonomy and control on the benefits of written emotion expression. *Personality & Social Psychology Bulletin, 35*(3), 351–364.

Wenger, E. (1998). *Communities of practice: Learning, meaning, and identity.* Cambridge, UK: Cambridge University Press.

Wentzel, K. R. (1997). Student motivation in middle school: The role of perceived pedagogical caring. *Journal of Educational Psychology, 89*(3), 411–419.

WhiteHouse.gov. (2014). Education: Knowledge and skills for the jobs of the future. Available at www.whitehouse.gov/issues/education/k-12/connected

Wood, D. J., Bruner, J. S., & Ross, G. (1976). The role of tutoring in problem solving. *Journal of Child Psychiatry and Psychology, 17*(2), 89–100.

Yamagata-Lynch, L. C. (2010). *Activity systems analysis methods: Understanding complex learning environments.* New York, NY: Springer.

Zhao, Y. (2012). *World class learners: Educating creative and entrepreneurial students.* Thousand Oaks, CA: Corwin Press. A joint publication with the National Association of Elementary School Principals.

Index

About the Author

Ed Madison is a seasoned media professional with a 30-year track record as an executive producer/director, entrepreneur, and innovative educator. His multifaceted career in media and journalism began as a high school intern at the *Washington Post*–owned CBS television affiliate in Washington, DC, during the height of Watergate. He has produced and directed programs and segments worldwide for network, syndicated, and cable television. Ed holds a Ph.D. in Communication from the School of Journalism and Communication at the University of Oregon (2012), where he is a tenure-track assistant professor and manages media partnerships. He teaches media innovation, multimedia journalism, and documentary filmmaking. He also teaches experimental courses in media and technology for UO's College of Education.

At age 22, Madison was recruited to become a founding producer for CNN, where he aided in creating groundbreaking quality programming that has come to represent that network. His own subsequent companies have provided services for most of the major networks and studios, including CBS, ABC, A&E, Paramount, Disney, and Discovery. He is an Apple Distinguished Educator and an Adobe Education Leader.

Ed is also founder of Media Arts Institute, a nonprofit organization committed to inspiring and educating digital learners and future generations of media professionals.

You can find updated resources and videos to accompany *Newsworthy* at NewsworthyBook.com.